This book belongs to

_____

. . . A WOMAN AFTER
GOD'S OWN *heart*

women

at the cross

Discovering the Work of the Cross in the Lives of
12 Women of the Bible – for Today's Woman

Mary Ellen Beachy

Women at the Cross

Mary Ellen Beachy

© Copyright Carlisle Press, January 2011

First Printing   July 2011   3 M
Second Printing   April 2013   2.5 M

ISBN 978.1.933753.17.1

Book Design by Abigail Troyer

Carlisle Press
WALNUT CREEK

2673 Township Road 421
Sugarcreek, OH 44681
1.800.852.4482

Dedicated

TO MY DAUGHTERS

Mary Lynita and Margretta Joy

Only a mother knows
How much she delights
In the life of her daughter,
Rejoices in her fresh young beauty,
Tries diligently to teach her
The skills she needs to be of service
And a blessing wherever she goes in life.
Oh yes, you, my daughter,
Are very, very precious;
I want you to know,
Whatever you do,
Wherever you go,
I will always pray for you;
I will always love you.

May God bless you,
May God keep you.
Always embrace the Cross of Christ
And live joyfully for Jesus,
Our King of Kings
And Lord of Lords.

Acknowledgments

To God

be all the glory for inspiration and ideas.

My husband

Mark, for his faithful love and support.

My daughters

Mary Lynita, for editing these pages. I greatly valued her encouragement. She has so much of what my English lacks.

Margretta Joy, for the times she said, "Mom, you just sit down and finish your writing projects. I'll do the ordinary work." What a blessing it was! She rolled up her sleeves and did it! Her fingers flew when she typed for me too.

My sons

Matthias: He could quickly help me figure out computer things, organize files, etc. Thanks!

Marcellus, Markus, and Micah: They make good writing material and keep our home lively.

I thank God for my own dear family.

My friends

Dianna, Delight, Faith, Ann, Sharon, Darlene, Ruby, and Miriam: Thank you for taking time to share your inspiring stories.

Foreword

"Now there stood by the cross of Jesus his mother, and his mother's sister, Mary the wife of Cleophas, and Mary Magdalene" (John 19:25).

This book is about women who came to the Cross, and continue daily to come to find purpose and meaning in life. My purpose for this book is to encourage ordinary women like myself.

- To search the Scriptures and see the dedication of godly women and the difference they made in the lives of their families and others in Bible times.
- To do your ordinary work "as unto the Lord," offering up yourself as a living daily sacrifice for Jesus.
- To be encouraged with the lives of men and women who lived their days with the passionate purpose to please the Lord.

Life is filled with many ordinary days and mountains of mundane work. There are spiritual battles for each woman of God.

Unless we meet Jesus at the Cross we are not ready to meet the challenges of life. The Cross of Jesus Christ is either our comfort or our condemnation. The Cross of Jesus Christ is our salvation. We must know the Lord of the Cross!!

The first part of each chapter is about a woman from the Bible. Then down-to-earth lessons to learn from her, and experiences from my life and the lives of others who have embraced the "Way of the Cross."

The story at the end of each chapter is about contemporary women whose lives are worthy to learn from and emulate.

Mary Ellen Beachy

Table of Contents

CHAPTER ONE

Blameless
and Barren

Elizabeth was a woman of a beautiful spirit; one who did not become bitter through the crushing disappointment of month after month, year after year of barrenness. She was faithful in ordinary days and sought God in all her ways. She chose to be grateful for the blessings that were hers.

Her life and home were peacefully quiet—too quiet. In years gone by, her intense heart's desire was to be blessed by God with children. How she had yearned for a son; not just one, but many sons and daughters. Tears—warm, wet tears—spilled down her cheeks. "Lord," she prayed, "I don't understand, but whatever You have for me, I want to embrace Your will."

More years went by, and still their home was silent. No sweet patter of lively feet, no joyous music of childish laughter and prattle. There was no small child to love and diligently teach for Jehovah God.

Elizabeth could not fathom why God would not answer her cries for a child. Her Jewish culture viewed fruitfulness as a great blessing and barrenness as a momentous reproach. A barren woman was often concluded to be guilty of some weighty sin, and therefore, Elizabeth suffered.

Through all the unfulfilled dreams, through the yearnings when she saw other women holding babies to their breasts, through all the rejection and whisperings, Elizabeth continued walking with God. Her utmost heart's desire was to do God's holy will. The passing of many years found her with a gentle radiance and a sweet spirit that permeated her life and blessed those she knew.

Her comfort and solace was God and His Holy Word. She learned to cast her burdens upon the Lord and He sustained her (Psalm 55:22).

Her other great comfort was her husband, Zacharias. Luke 1:6 says, "They were both righteous before God, walking in all the commandments and ordinances of the Lord blameless." Theirs was an enviable testimony. Together, they sought God and served Him. They were dedicated, devoted, and diligent as they daily walked with God. Theirs was not just a Sunday religion. They lived honestly before God and man, equitable in character.

They were devoted to God, even though these were dark days in Israel. Truly, the scepter had departed from Judah. For the first time, the throne was filled by a non-Jew. They were enslaved by the Romans. Herod the Great, though an able ruler, was brutally ruthless and cruel. Even Jehovah God had been silent in Palestine for four hundred dark years.

In the midst of all this darkness, the lives of Zacharias and Elizabeth shone like glowing candles. They clung to their faith in God. They had grown old, but they had not grown bitter and cynical.

Little did Zacharias and Elizabeth know that Jehovah God was about to bless their lives with an astounding, amazing surprise—a miracle that would be a blessing of joy and gladness to their home, and to countless others.

Their dreams for a son were dead, for Elizabeth was now past child-bearing age. Yet, God knew their home was ready to raise a man for Him. Their holy living, faithfulness, and fervent prayers had prepared them to be used by God. To accomplish His work in His perfect timing, God would perform a miracle.

Your Prayers Are Heard

On that eventful day, Zacharias was responsible to attend to the burning of incense in the temple. The priests offered the burnt offerings and the incense offering simultaneously every day. Incense was an emblem of the prayers and praise of the people of God. The smoke of the incense mingled with the smoke of the sacrifice.

The time spent in burning incense was likely thirty minutes, during which the people maintained a reverent, profound silence as they prayed. The smoke of the incense and the prayers of the people were ascending up to God. They were praying, pleading, and imploring God to remember them and send the Messiah.

What a perfect time for the angel to come with the wondrous message for Zacharias. But Zacharias was startled and filled with fear at the presence of the angel on the right side of the altar of incense. God did not leave him troubled, for the angel said, "Fear not, Zacharias, thy prayer is heard. Your wife Elizabeth shall bear thee a son. Thou shalt have joy and gladness, and many shall rejoice at his birth. Thou shalt call his name John. He shall be great in the sight of the Lord, and filled with the Holy Ghost, even from his mother's womb. He shall turn many of the children of Israel to the Lord their God, to make ready a people prepared for the Lord" (Luke 1:13-17).

God had spoken! The four hundred years of silence were broken! "Zacharias, your prayers are heard; the long-awaited answer is here at last. Your prayers for a son, your prayers for the deliverance and consolation of Israel, your prayers and pleadings, they are all heard!" Unfortunately, Zacharias doubted the angel's words. "How can this be?" he questioned, "for my wife and I are now old."

The angel spoke again, saying, "I am Gabriel, that stand in the presence of God; and am sent to speak unto thee, and to shew thee these glad tidings. And, behold, thou shalt be dumb, and not able to speak, until the day that these things shall be performed, because thou believest not my words, which shall be fulfilled in their season" (Luke 1:19, 20).

ELIZABETH'S RESPONSE

In your mind's eye, picture a man who could not speak, writing such a life-changing message to the woman he loved. "Elizabeth, an angel spoke to me. God is going to give us a son!"

What was her response? "Thus hath the Lord dealt with me in the days wherein he looked on me," she exclaimed, "to take away my reproach among men" (Luke 1:25).

Elizabeth rejoiced at the wonderful news. She was filled with the Spirit of God; her focus was on God. She had an overwhelming sense of gratitude and praise, rather than the spirit of grievance. She did not focus on why this did not take place many years before.

After she conceived the child, she went into seclusion for five months. Imagine the silence. Who did she talk with when her husband couldn't talk? I believe she spent much time in prayer, conversing with God, and seeking God's will in His Word.

Elizabeth lived up to her lovely name which means, "God is my oath" or "a worshiper of God." She did what each godly woman needs to do, and wants to do. She sought God for wisdom to teach and train the special child God would give to them.

One day, there was a knock at Elizabeth's door. God sent to her house a golden blessing, a lovely maiden to brighten and bless the last three months of her pregnancy.

Is your situation today similar to Elizabeth's? Your arms are empty and you yearn for and pray for a child?

Or are you already a busy mother, and know that God is sending you yet another little one? You wonder how you will ever be able to cope. How will you manage more duties?

Or, you may be single, lonely, and longing for the love and companionship of a husband. Does it seem as though day after day goes by in a dull way, and nothing exciting or unusual ever happens to you? Whatever your lot in life, you need:

· Trust and faith
· Gratitude
· Love for children

Trust and Faith

"Earth is for trust, heaven is for understanding."

Just think, the same God who heard and answered Zacharias and Elizabeth's prayers is our God today! Do I really believe God's words and promises in difficult times?

Because of Zacharias' unbelief, silence was imposed on him by the Lord. Until the power that silenced him gave him permission to speak again, he was unable to break that silence. Imagine nine months of silence for one intemperate speech.

Today, we can lose our praise and thanksgiving for months or even years when we give in to the language of unbelief. Elizabeth testified in Luke 1:45, "Blessed (happy) is she who believes."

The Jewish culture highly valued having children, so much so that some said barrenness gave a man grounds for divorce. Imagine the blessing and honor Zacharias and Elizabeth would have missed had Zacharias divorced his lovely wife because she was barren. Would God have blessed Elizabeth with a child if she had become bitter in her barrenness?

Today, have courage. Take heart. Be faithful. Wholeheartedly do the work God has given you to do. Love Him more. Search and study His Word more. Then you will be ready and prepared (as Zacharias and Elizabeth were) for whatever God has for you.

God rewards those who faithfully keep on trusting and doing His will in difficult days.

Gratitude

"What a blessing it is to make gratitude a daily attitude."

One day, Elsie Beachy was struck with a strange malady that eventually put her in a wheelchair. "I had to finally accept my condition, or drown in the misery of self-pity," Elsie said. "If God wants to use me as a handicapped wife, a handicapped grandmother, I will do my best for Him."

When we were in their area for school meetings, we spent the night at Ivan and Elsie's house. As I walked into her kitchen that morning, she sat in her wheelchair, sweeping her floor and singing. I just stood there in amazement, watching.

Her testimony spoke loudly. Am I thankful that I can work? Every day my floors need to be swept. I can be thankful I can do my mundane duties "as unto the Lord," or I can sigh and complain about all the work and the dirt.

"She looketh well to the ways of her household" (Proverbs 31:27). These words often ring through my mind as I sweep my kitchen floor. God cares about all the ordinary work a woman is called to do.

A young man said he was attracted to his girlfriend by her grateful spirit. She was always finding something to be thankful for. Who wouldn't enjoy living with a woman like that!

Consider the blessings of developing a grateful heart:
· Thankfulness pleases God.
· Thankful people are as a refreshing drink of cool water.
· Everyone enjoys being with a grateful person.

A grateful, merry heart spills over into our children's lives, and gives them more sunshine. What is our response when they have a childish accident like spilling water or breaking a dish? My sister-in-law Faith remarked that her ten-year-old daughter dumped a bucket of slop on the kitchen floor. She had the choice to scold and fuss, or to laugh and be kind. Faith had the grace to laugh, and made no big deal out of the mess. Can you imagine the difference that choice made in the atmosphere of her home?

Love for Children

"He treasures little children."

There is such a stark contrast between the kingdom of God and the kingdom of Satan. God's kingdom is full of light, love, warmth, and peace; Satan's is full of darkness, and is sinister and cruel.

Consider the difference in the way the two kingdoms value children and sweet, innocent babies. Jesus took time for children. He loved them and blessed them. The beautiful lyrics of this song call us to do likewise.

Suffer the Children to Come

Hark! I hear my Savior say, "Suffer the children to come to me."
Do not turn the lambs away, "Suffer the children to come."
Point them to the Father's throne, speak to them in tend'rest tone,
Jesus calls them for His own, "Suffer the children to come."

Chorus:
Do not turn the lambs away, precious in His sight are they;
Teach them how to watch and pray, "Suffer the children to come."

Tell them Jesus loves them all, "Suffer the children to come to me."
He will guide them lest they fall, "Suffer the children to come."
Oh, forbid them not, I pray, precious in His sight are they,
Teach them how to watch and pray, "Suffer the children to come."

Take them gently by the hand, "Suffer the children to come to me."
Lead them to the better land, "Suffer the children to come."
Lead them with a willing mind, tell them of a Savior kind,
They eternal life may find, "Suffer the children to come."

Do we take time to bless the children in our lives?

One winter day, my three-year-old son went out with me to gather the eggs. A thick blanket of snow covered the ground. On impulse he said, "Let's walk to the creek!" Why shouldn't I take time to do that? We went, hand in hand.

Happily we chattered, "Isn't this snow beautiful? I'm glad God made white snow."

Walks are such an excellent time to talk to our little ones about God and His marvelous creation. Twice, on the way back, Micah ran ahead, then he would run back to me, small arms outstretched, eager to be swooped up in a warm hug.

We never will regret time spent in brightening and blessing our children's days. Some days, though, it is much easier said than done.

On a damp, cold, dreary day in December, my mood matched

the weather. I was starting with a head cold, and my back ached. When evening came, I longed to put up my feet by the hearth and relax in peace and quiet. But that evening, Mark was scheduled to go caroling with his students. He left, leaving me with five lively children. We had delicious chicken noodle soup for dinner; however, it is not the children's favorite. I told them quite sternly to eat it without grumbling if they want dessert. The evening went well. I read to the little boys, and we played games. However, I realized that I should have been more pleasant.

The next morning, I discovered a school paper Matthias (11) had written. This is what it said. "My mom's name is Mary Ellen. She is kind, patient, and loving. She likes to sing at breakfast so we don't argue. She was born in Maryland. She has 2 sisters and 5 brothers. Now she has 2 girls and 4 boys. She is very content."

That knocked me over the head. I felt unworthy. I had been especially irked at the boys' noises and attitudes the evening before. I knew I had apologies to make.

Words from a song ran through my mind, "Don't give up, try again."

Titus 2:4 states that young women are to love their husband and their children. We need God's help to do that consistently. I ask God to help me to love my husband and children always. Our families are priceless and precious.

In contrast, there has never been a child Satan didn't despise. He was killing babies to kill Moses. He was destroying infants to destroy Christ. His tactics haven't changed. Millions of babies are still aborted; thousands of children are abused. Jesus said of Satan, "He was a murderer from the beginning" (John 8:44).

In the ancient Greek world of Ephesus, there were thousands of prostitutes. When a woman gave birth, she would look at the baby and decide whether or not she would keep the child. All the unwanted babies were laid at the dump by one of the city gates. There may have been a hundred unwanted babies a day. In the morning, slave merchants would pick through those babies. They chose the strongest and best looking. How horrible! Yet in our culture today, women by the millions choose to abort their unplanned, unwanted babies. Someday, each of us will give account to God for the deeds we have done. Are we counted with those who love and bless children, or do we turn the lambs away?

Learning from John the Baptist

Parents greatly impact their children's lives. In the end, their lives and examples teach louder than any other influence.

Zacharias and Elizabeth were a shining example of righteousness before God, walking in His commandments and ordinances blameless. They left a profound example of godliness. Now, like the parents, so is their son.

Seven Lessons from John the Baptist's Life

1. He knew his life's purpose and faithfully fulfilled it (John 1:23). Do I faithfully carry out what I know is God's will for me each day? If the purpose of your life were expressed in one sentence, what might it be?

2. He was totally dedicated and earnest, giving his best, his all (Matthew 3:1-3). His crying voice denotes earnestness. Am I a lukewarm or a wholehearted Christian? Do I truly love my husband and children and take my responsibilities seriously?

3. He did not hesitate to speak the truth. He was not afraid to speak out against sin (Mark 6:18). Am I afraid to stand alone on Christian principles? Am I willing to live and die for obedience to the truth?

4. He was humble and meek, willing to have Jesus increase and himself decrease (John 1:27-30, Matthew 3:11). Do I give God the glory for all good in my life? Or do I endeavor to exalt myself?

5. He was a just and a holy man (Mark 6:20). Holy: he walked and talked with God, and was just in his dealings with man. Do I walk and talk with God each day? Do I focus on His approval? Am I honest?

6. A man of steadiness and consistency, he was not afraid to stand alone (Luke 7:24-26). Do I know what I believe and why?

7. He was a man of unparalleled self-denial (Mark 1:6). His dress and diet spoke of poverty, simplicity, and humility. Am I willing to deny myself questionable, debatable things of the world to be obedient to God and to support my church? Am I willing to deny myself things for the good of my children? (Things such as television, questionable music, electronic baby-sitters, and modern entertainments.) Am I willing to deny myself fashions that violate God's principles of modesty?

· ·

This chapter closes with a story about Mary Martha Miller. She, like Elizabeth, was a woman with a wholehearted passion for God. Unlike Elizabeth, God gave her nine children. Twins died in infancy.

Mary Martha left a profound influence for godliness on the lives of her family. Her heart and home were open to others who needed God's love as well. Her prayer life and her hospitality on the prairies of Kansas were extraordinary.

· ·

"The most important work you and I will ever do will be within the walls of our own homes."

—*Harold B. Lee*

Choosing Gratefulness
Mary Martha (Nisly) Miller, 1919-2007

—Miriam Iwashige

Mary Martha Nisly skipped along beside her sister Matilda on their way to the barn. Milking time had arrived. Mary would have to watch today, but she was almost eight, and then she would be allowed to help. Dad didn't allow loud, boisterous laughter, but Alma, Ora, Matilda, and Dad's singing made the barn a happy place at milking time, and Mary wanted to be part of the fun. Times were good.

Just beyond the horizon lurked two momentous events for Mary's family. Within three years, the whole country was plunged into a major Depression. Abraham (Abie) and Sarah, Mary's parents, often didn't know if they could keep their home and farm operation together. On one of their rare trips to town, Mary saw her mother count out coins at the bank till she had enough to cover the $20.00 they owed for the month's rent. With food from the farm and garden, the family did not go hungry, even though they were desperately short of cash.

But far worse than the Depression was Matilda's sudden death from an intestinal obstruction. On May 29, 1926, at age eleven, she died during surgery. She had been such a sunny child and a little mother to her younger siblings. Her death plunged the family into deep grief. Singing in the barn was hard without Matilda. Springtime was never the same after that.

Alma and Dorothy were pretty like Matilda had been, and Esther and Viola were cute. But Mary did not feel pretty. She felt sure she would never get married because of it. At least she would not be ugly *and* slow and grouchy. She was working on being grateful; she loved school and did well. She could work hard and fast, and she could sing like Grandpa Nisly. Her diligence paid off at the end of eighth grade when all the students in public schools in the county took the same test to measure their achievement. Mary's score was the third highest in the county.

Mary was wrong about one thing. When she was 23, Ervin Miller from Oklahoma became her husband. Before they were married, he heard his employer's family talking about the fair in Hutchinson and a cooking contest that was part of it. They thought that if Mary and her sisters entered the contest, they would easily win. Ervin was pleased to hear others affirm what he already believed—that Mary would make a lovely wife.

Ervin and Mary's December wedding day was beautiful—warm enough to have the windows open. She had prayed for a nice day, and had bargained with God that she would never complain about the weather if He would grant her request. Her children vouch for the fact that she kept her word.

Mary cooked for Ervin for almost 60 years, along with many, many meals for invited guests, boarders, employees, and a growing family. While her daughter Lillian was growing up, she remembers spending long hours with food preparation, and then feeling dismay at how fast it disappeared when the hungry crowd descended on it. But Mary loved to see people enjoy her food. In her hands, a glass of milk and a bottle of chocolate syrup became a rich brown treat for grandson Gerald, as a small reward for carrying in the groceries. He reports that her Rice Krispie candy had more marshmallows in it than was good for anyone.

Generous giver as she was, Mary still loved to be thanked. She once responded wistfully to her son Harold's thanks after a meal, when seed house workers and all others had disappeared, by asking, "Where are the nine?"

Ervin and Mary began their life together living with Mary's parents. Alma was born during this time. Mary's youngest brother Paul, who was only three years old, still remembers the happy day when Mary and the new baby arrived home from the hospital in an ambulance from Hutchinson, 18 miles away. It would have been too far to drive in a jolting buggy with a new mother and baby.

When Alma was four months old, the family moved to a small house on a farm about three miles away. They rented the house from the Russells, and lived in this small house for the next 24 years.

Life in the little house began happily enough, but in 1944, after Ervin and Mary had lived in their own house for about a year, Mary gave birth to premature twins, Paul Jay and Pauline Mae, who weighed only a little over three pounds each. They were born by emergency Caesarean Section and both died within the first 24 hours. Kind hands made tiny clothes for the babies' burial. Ervin stayed at Mary's side in the hospital while others held a graveside service for the babies that Mary already loved, but would never care for. In later years, she seldom spoke of the twins, perhaps because she wanted to spare her children the grieving she remembered enduring after Matilda's death.

Mary herself was gravely ill after the twins' birth. She received a blood transfusion because of hemorrhaging and then contracted yellow jaundice, possibly caused by hepatitis from tainted blood. For 30 days, she stayed in the hospital, part of that time hovering precariously between life and death. "We gave her enough medicine to kill a horse," her doctor said, regarding the intensive treatment she received. During this time, one-year-old Alma stayed with Mary's parents. Her young aunts doted on her and called her Princess, a name one of them used for her into Alma's adulthood.

When Glenn was born later, also by C-section, medical protocol decreed the family complete. Women were advised to not have more than two C-sections, and having babies naturally after a C-section was thought to be too risky. But Ervin and Mary longed for more children. Mary begged for Dr. Barnes' cooperation. She was willing to take on the medical risks if her doctor would agree to continue caring for her. Her doctor agreed. When the next child was born naturally, they named him Harold, also Dr. Barnes' given name. Throughout the next years, LaVerne, Marvin, Loren, and Lillian were born in that order, with no life-threatening complications. However, Dr. Barnes declared before

Lillian's birth that this one would be a C-section. "We've taken enough risks," he said.

The two-bedroom house expanded by one bedroom to accommodate the growing family, but Mrs. Russell refused to allow any more additions to the house. The boys' small room had a double bed and one single bed. All five boys slept there. The girls' room was for Alma, and later, Lillian.

In 1964, when Alma got married, she was hardly out the door to go live with her new husband when some of her brothers began moving into her old bedroom. Little Lillian was relegated to the living room sofa, and slept there the rest of the time they lived in that house. The house was very crowded, but whenever Ervin or the children seemed troubled by these circumstances, Mary would say, "I need no mansion here below," quoting the words from a song, and echoing the sentiments of Scripture.

During the busy years of raising a family, Mary worked extremely hard, rising as early as 2:00 on Monday mornings to get the laundry done. For years, her regular rising time was 4:00 AM. Daybreak found her working in the garden during the growing season. She often said in German, "*Die Morgen Stund hat Gold im Mund.*" (The morning hour has gold in its mouth.) Mary must have prayed much during these early morning hours of working alone. After the noon meal, she usually took a nap, and saw to it that her young children did too. They were not allowed to stay up late, and were often headed for bed around 7:00.

Although Mary's physical crises had subsided, other challenges loomed large. Ervin worked very hard to provide well financially for his family, but sometimes felt thwarted by circumstances beyond his control. The fledgling seed cleaning business Ervin and Mary had started in 1947 on the farm held no guarantee of success. A three-year drought began in 1952, and farm income was sparse during this time. Ervin was often deeply discouraged and sometimes had difficulty relating well to others outside the family. Mary's generous, easily placated spirit must have grieved during such times. She did all she could to smooth over the rough spots, without ever being disparaging or complaining. Others noticed this and admired her.

Some of Mary's children were especially strong-willed, and all of them needed appropriate direction. She was firm, but her children do not remember ever being chastened in anger. My mother remembers teaching one of her sons in Bible school. He was not happy with the part he had been assigned for the Bible school program. When Mary caught wind of the situation, she asked questions of my mother till she was sure she knew what his teacher wanted of him. "He'll do it," she informed my mother resolutely. He did, with no further complaint.

As a young child, Loren, on his way to the bathroom at 4:00 one morning, found his mother at the sewing machine with her Bible open. "What are you doing, Mama?" he asked.

"I'm praying," she answered.

"What are you praying about?" he wondered.

"I have five boys, and I don't know how to raise them. I'm asking God to show me," Mary replied.

She often sang as she worked, and prayed much that her children would learn to love to sing. When the children worked with her, she would often tell them stories—stories with lessons she never failed to point out, although she was careful not to mention names if the story reflected negatively on anyone. Later, Glenn grinned to himself when he heard some of the same stories from an acquaintance. She told them with no shame. They were about her own family. Some of the identity mysteries were solved, despite Mary's watchful integrity.

Ervin and Mary's family had daily devotions together. Each day, they usually read several chapters in the Bible. Mary recorded on the flyleaf of her Bible what books they had read through—some of them many times—by the time the family was grown. During the early years, they read in German, so the children would learn that language well. And they always sang. As the family matured, the boys wanted to learn new songs, so singing a new song from the hymnal they used in church became a daily part of family devotions.

Mary helped with farm work when necessary, even occasionally doing field work with the tractor. Often with just a moment's notice, she hurried to town for parts when the farm equipment broke down.

Grocery shopping happened at a fast clip, and Mary's sons remember struggling to keep up with her. She always walked fast. The minutes were precious. Everywhere she went, if there was a chance of a little waiting time, she had a project at hand—in the doctor's office waiting room: writing a letter, or, Bible and commentary in hand, she studied in preparation for teaching her current Sunday school class. Young and old liked her for a teacher, even if she required lots of Bible memory work. If she was at home while studying, she frequently consulted a dictionary to make sure that her spelling and pronunciation were correct. Slipshod work would never do. Anyone who received a gift from her saw evidence of this in the way she marked the gift with the date and the recipient's name.

Mary always loved to read, and many of the most memorable things she came across were for a time displayed under the glass on the desk, and found their way into her conversations. Over her kitchen sink, she posted the verses in Psalm 90:10&12. "The days of our years are threescore years and ten; and if by reason of strength they be fourscore years, yet is their strength labour and sorrow; for it is soon cut off, and we fly away. So teach us to number our days, that we may apply our hearts unto wisdom."

Pithy sayings sprang easily to her lips, and her children remember many of them. "Two wrongs never make a right," she would say if one of her children felt mistreated and wanted things set right, by whatever means necessary. "Cleanliness is next to godliness," was a maxim she lived by. When something particularly impressed her, she said, "I don't think I'll forget that as long as I have a good mind," and she prayed that her mind would last as long as her body. Sometimes she reminded others that a good mind was a gift from God, and telling stories in jest about someone not blessed with a good mind was unacceptable. "I want to sleep tonight," she would say as an explanation for why she needed to do the right thing, regardless. She stressed the importance of maintaining personal purity. Her scrupulous honesty extended to depositing back in the coin slot a dime returned in error at a phone booth in Saint Louis while they were traveling.

Her home ministers remember that she paid strict attention to each sermon and took careful notes. If she missed getting something written down, she often inquired afterwards so that she could complete her outline. Visiting ministers also often heard a word of appreciation from her.

In about 1966, Ervin and Mary were able to buy the farm they lived on, and they soon began to build a new house. By piping water from a better well they dug more than one and one-half miles away, they found a way to address the chronic problems with their meager and salty water supply. Also, close to the new house was a pond that filled up when nearby Sugar Creek flowed strong after good rains. They irrigated from the pond, and planted trees and grass and flowers, over time being rewarded with a lush and colorful landscape in that windswept place. Mary cherished this beauty denied her during earlier years because of the water problems, and nurtured the vegetation carefully. When a visitor commented on the beautiful grapevine twining through the wrought iron along the porch in front of the house, she informed him that God had planted that vine. "You mean the birds planted it."

"No. I mean God planted it."

The roomy new house had space for boarders. One troubled young man, who had never lived at any one place very long as an adult, stayed in their home for several years. Another fellow was from Poland, part of an international trainee exchange program. He stayed for six months, the allotted time allowed by the program he was part of. During the busy season at the seed house, employees from out of state sometimes came to help. They too lived with Ervin and Mary's family. Clearly, hospitality was not only a Sunday dinner tradition in this household.

The early '70s were heady times for Kansas farmers, when a new trade agreement with Russia drove the wheat price up higher than ever, and bankers encouraged expansion. However, commodity prices dropped catastrophically in the '80s, and many farmers found themselves in dire straits, Ervin and Mary among them. If Mary had been a chronic worrier, these financial uncertainties would likely have been overwhelming. As it was, after painstaking planning and negotiation, some of the farmland was sold, the bank shared some of the losses, and foreclosure was averted. The farm operation eventually recovered. Mary's lifetime practice of courage and optimism did not fail her in this crisis.

In 1982, Mary was driving their farm pickup on a country road when she had a serious accident. Unknown to her, some of the dirt over a culvert under the roadway had washed out, and one truck wheel dropped into the gaping hole, causing her to lose control. The vehicle veered off the road and hit the exposed end of a second culvert under a field drive just beyond the pothole. My sister Dorcas, one of the seed house employees, was with her, and ended up on the floor of the truck, under the dash, but was not badly hurt.

Mary walked out with no visible injuries, but the steering wheel had jabbed hard into her abdomen. The lady who carried the mail came upon the accident very shortly, and insisted that Mary get into her car so that she could take her home. Mary was quite sure she was fine, but did as Mrs. Stiggins urged. When they arrived at the Miller home several miles away, Mrs. Stiggins told Ervin and Glenn that Mary was fading fast, and needed to get to a hospital. Mary declared she was just in shock and wanted to go to the house to lie down, but Glenn took one look at the mail lady's face and his mother's face and swung into action. He guided her to the back seat of their car and Ervin joined her. Glenn drove as fast as he dared toward the hospital. Ervin thought it was still too slow. They arrived with no time to spare. Mary was bleeding internally from a torn spleen and badly damaged liver. She had surgery almost immediately, facilitated by the fact that the accident happened on Mary's weekly fast day, and her stomach was empty. The doctor said she would not have lasted five minutes more without treatment—much more time than would have been lost if they had waited for an ambulance. During the two weeks in the Intensive Care Unit, her life again hung in the balance for some time. She begged God to allow her to die.

While Mary was in the hospital, a family member at home continued to struggle with depression. When things got more desperate than ever during this time, Mary could not help, even if she had known exactly what to do. Everything was beyond her control.

Mary understood eventually that God would give her grace to face life again, rather than remove her from it. Due to injuries along her spine, she never had a pain-free day for the rest of her 24 years of life, but whenever anyone asked her how she was, she would answer, "Grateful."

"No, I mean, really, how do you feel?"

"I have so much to be thankful for."

"You're not answering my question."

"Well, I always have pain, but God is good."

As long as she was physically able, she made it a point to visit an ill or needy person on the anniversary of her accident, in gratitude for her own life having been spared.

With professional help and medical treatment, the family member's depression lifted. But for Mary, more hurdles remained.

Some of Mary's grandchildren were born with serious hearing impairments. Mary did not minimize the seriousness of this challenge, but chose to affirm the Lord's hand in it by quoting Exodus 4:11: " ...Who hath made man's mouth? Or who maketh the dumb, or deaf, or the seeing, or the blind? Have not I the Lord?"

When a ten-month-old grandson living in another state died suddenly of meningitis, Ervin and Mary returned home from the child's funeral with crushed hearts. Because public statements from law enforcement had called some of the actions of the child's father into question, he had been taken into custody. Facing people seemed impossible, and they could not imagine that anything but rejection awaited them. But they attended church as always, and, as they testified later, were overwhelmed with the warm reception they received from their church family. Mary did not miss the opportunity to examine her own heart at this time of crisis. At some point, she confessed in church having had family pride. People who heard her speak were awed at this woman's courage.

Within the next few years, her son Loren, who then had a wife and three young children, suffered critical injuries in a traffic accident on an icy road. Most of the bones on one side of his body were broken. He suffered brain injury, and barely hung on to life in the fog of a prolonged medically-induced coma. Very slowly, he regained a measure of good health and normal function, and his cognitive powers began to return.

In 1997, Mary had surgery to replace a faulty heart valve. It was a major faith-stretching experience and she prepared for the prospect of not surviving the surgery. She did recover well. In 1998, she had cataract surgery and a knee replacement. In 1999, the other knee was replaced. A stroke followed in 2000, after which she regained mobility, but never recovered completely. After a final surgery in 2005 to remove a bone spur in her knee, her physical health declined markedly. Her earlier determination to do whatever was necessary to recover fast from surgery failed her, and she needed encouragement to continue therapy. She still longed for heaven, but seemed resigned to leaving the timing in God's hands. "I'm tired and I'm ready to go," she told John Davies, a former neighbor who had come back to the area for a visit and saw her with Ervin at the gas pump in Partridge.

At the age of 88, Mary died quietly, in bed in her own home. Early in the morning Ervin had just brought her a drink and then gone to take a shower. When he returned to the bedroom, she was gone.

With a host of family members and friends present and helping, Mary's body was buried. Her son Marvin came from Romania and her daughter Lillian from El Salvador. Some of the El Salvador grandchildren, a grandson in Thailand, and another in Bangladesh could not make the trip. But there were great-grandchildren there, and even small ones helped by gathering up stray dirt clods and adding them to the growing pile over the grave.

Today (2008), Alma, Glenn, and LaVerne live in Kansas. Alma is married to Edward Miller, who has been the treasurer for the Center Church for decades. Four of their six children are teachers. Glenn and his wife Anna operate a bulk food and Gospel book store at Pleasantview, the hub of the Amish and Mennonite community in central Reno County. They attend the local Amish church. Their children are now serving or have in the past served in Latin America and several Asian countries. Three of their four sons work as computer programmers, and the other as a "tentmaker" missionary. LaVerne, married to Rebecca, is a deacon in the Center Amish Mennonite Church where Ervin and Mary attended and where their children grew up. He also continues with the farming and seed farm business. Several of their children have their sights set on cross-cultural missions.

Loren and Harold live elsewhere in the United States. Loren, married to Dolores, directs a Christian ministry in Colorado that serves incarcerated mothers by caring for their babies. Harold lives in Pennsylvania with his wife Ruth, where he teaches school and does market gardening. He has had a decades-long constituency-wide-and-beyond ministry related to Christian music.

Marvin and Lillian are missionaries. Marvin and his wife Ruth have been involved for a number of years in a ministry in Romania. Lillian and her husband Arthur Nisly have a home in El Salvador, where they have raised their family and where they have a personal, long-term commitment to live and serve. These faraway offspring of Ervin and Mary also have children who assist in their parents' ministry.

Ervin is still involved in farming. In recent years, he has promised that he will retire when he turns 90 on July 4, 2008. Wheat harvest may still be in progress then, and it would be out of character for Ervin not to participate. Time will tell.

During the last 24 years of Mary's life, she saw many of her prayers answered, and rejoiced in many blessings. Although her vigor declined greatly in the last few years, and she never prepared a meal after her stroke in 2000, she was able to attend church services till the very last Sunday before she died. What she could not do for herself, her devoted family gladly did. Each of her 46 grandchildren and 33 great-grandchildren were precious to her. While the twins born to her did not survive, her descendants now include seven sets of twins, three of them grandchildren and four of them great-grandchildren. Her children grew up to love singing, and made serving the Lord a priority. All of them are useful in the Lord's work, and the grandchildren who are old enough to choose are following suit.

At Mary Martha's funeral, her younger brother, Paul, spoke of his sister and the appropriateness of the name her parents chose for her, a name she treasured. Like Martha, she served diligently and well in practical ways, and like Mary, she listened to and adored her Lord. Many friends, although not observing these things up close, sensed her abiding faith in the good hand of God, and knew her as an incurably grateful person.

She is in glory, but those of us here who struggle with any number of challenges can look at Mary's life and find a worthy example to follow. What a legacy!

CHAPTER TWO

Mother of the Messiah

M ary. Her life leaves us a lovely example of submission to the will of the Father.

God chose one family, one woman, through whom His only begotten Son would come to the land of the shadow of death, our earth. His Son would appear, a great Light to dispel the darkness.

What character traits would the woman who would be chosen to mother the Son of God possess?

There are days that change one's life forever. Such was the day when the angel Gabriel came to Mary with the astounding news that she was to be the mother of the Messiah. Among thousands of Jewish girls, why was Mary chosen?

"You are highly favored Mary; the Lord is with thee. Blessed art thou among women." That was Gabriel's message.

Mary could not comprehend what the angel meant. She was troubled.

Gabriel reassured her with the gracious words, "Fear not, Mary, you have found favor with God. You will conceive and bring forth a son. You are to call His name Jesus. He will be great, the Son of the Most High God. He will reign over the house of Jacob: His kingdom shall never end."

Mary, Pious and Pure

Mary wondered how she, a pure, chaste virgin, could conceive a child?

"With God nothing shall be impossible," said the angel Gabriel.

"Miraculous" describes the birth of Mary's child. She was told that Jesus Christ would be conceived by an action of God's Holy Spirit. There was no human father.

Mary, Sweet Submission

Mary's beautiful response signified a life in tune with the Father. "I am the Lord's servant," she said. "I am willing to do whatever He wants."

To be chosen, to find favor with God, was a position of great honor. Yet Mary was also quietly accepting a situation that was bound to cause scandal and storms. She possessed a gentle and quiet spirit, which is of great worth in God's sight (I Peter 3:4). Her trust in God was implicit.

Because she was chosen to be the mother of the Messiah, she suffered many dark moments and days of pain. Imagine, even Joseph, her beloved and betrothed, did not understand what was happening. He did not really believe Mary's words, and was contemplating to quietly break off their engagement.

What about her parents? They must have been God fearing and God honoring to have raised such an exemplary daughter. We are not told whether they understood or believed Mary when she told them of the angel's visit. However they responded, Mary's parents suffered with her through all the whisperings and wild rumors about Mary's condition.

In those days, pregnancy and sexual relationships out of wedlock were an awful disgrace. Under the Old Testament law, it was a sin punishable by stoning. God said, "So shalt thou put away evil from among you" (Deuteronomy 22:24b). Regardless of how the world today views it, sexual relationships outside of marriage are still wrong in the eyes of God. Be not deceived; God is not mocked. He calls us to lives of purity and holiness.

Although it seems that most people did not believe Mary's story, God did not leave her to suffer alone and unprotected. The Lord said to Joseph in a dream, "Do not be afraid to take Mary as your wife. That which is conceived of her is of the Holy Ghost."

Joseph believed, obeyed, and took Mary to be his wife. What a wonderful provision from God! Joseph loved, cared for, and provided for Mary! What joy and profound relief flooded Mary's whole being. Joseph's actions at such a critical time in her life evoked in her an intense love and appreciation for him. Always, she would love and cherish Joseph, her husband, provider, and leader.

Joseph and Mary's relationship was based on mutual commitment and obedience to God. There is no better foundation for a marriage.

Before her marriage, Mary had flown to her cousin Elizabeth's door. God knew where to send her to find the affirmation, acceptance, and approval she craved and needed. She and Elizabeth were both expecting miracle babies.

Oh, the unspeakable comfort in being loved, believed, and understood! Elizabeth said to Mary, "How is this that the mother of my Lord should come to me? Blessed are you among women, and blessed is the fruit of your womb."

MARY, A LOVER OF GOD

"My soul doth magnify the Lord," Mary responded. "My spirit hath rejoiced in God my Savior. God is mighty; holy is His name; He hath done great things to me." Truly, Mary loved and praised the Lord her God.

MARY, A LOVER OF THE WORD OF GOD

Mary's magnificat is full of echoes from the Scriptures. It includes fifteen quotations from the Old Testament, words Mary had known and loved since childhood.

The books of the Old Testament were the only books used in the Jewish synagogue schools. In Galilee, boys and girls went to school. Boys studied the Torah. Girls studied Psalms, Proverbs, Deuteronomy, and maybe Leviticus. We assume that Mary attended one of these schools.[1] Mary was well versed in the Word of God.

Mary stayed with Elizabeth for three months. I can imagine Mary, Elizabeth, and Zacharias poring over the Old Testament prophecies in the cool of the evening. "The Lord himself shall give you a sign; Behold, a virgin shall conceive and bear a son, and shall call his name Immanuel" (Isaiah 7:14). The Word ministered strength and assurance to Mary's soul.

These were days of preparation for future trials. Together, Mary and Elizabeth praised God, and prayed that they would have the faith and fortitude to fulfill their roles in God's amazing salvation plan.

When faith is put to the test, God often brings another person into the picture in a very meaningful way to strengthen both. The faith of these two lovely women, Mary and Elizabeth, reinforced each other.

THE MESSIAH'S BIRTH

God knows our need of enough sunshine to nourish our souls; enough storms to help us realize how desperately we need Him.

Imagine the difficulty of traveling one hundred miles, by foot or by donkey, just prior to giving birth. Then, upon arrival, there was no room for them in decent lodging. No room except in a lowly stable. Had God forgotten them?

Yet there was that awesome, supernatural announcement to the shepherds. The angelic choir proclaiming the birth of Christ the Lord brought great comfort and joy to the hearts of Joseph and Mary. Mary quietly pondered all these things in her heart. Her belief in God was the firm anchor that held her up through all these strange and wonderful happenings.

The mysterious visit of the wise men and their rich gifts sustained the little family through the dark and stormy flight to Egypt. Surely, they heard of the massacre from which they had escaped in Bethlehem. Mary pondered on this, too.

How many years were Mary, Joseph, and Jesus in Egypt? Though they deeply cherished family connections, their time in Egypt enhanced their cleaving to each other and to God.

Did their family and friends welcome them back home with open arms when they finally returned to Nazareth? What a relief to come home again, yet there always loomed over them the whispers, the dark shadows of those who never believed; those who considered Jesus to be an illegitimate son. Later in Jesus' ministry, He could not do many mighty works in Nazareth.

Nazareth
He was a prophet without honor here,
Here where His boyish feet had flung the sand.
He read the message in the passing leer
And grin, "Who does He think He is, this Son of Joseph?"
Faces stirred with quiet smirks,
He paused beside the home gate, thinking on
The places that had seen His mighty works.
And here in his hometown, He saw with grief
All miracles stillborn because of unbelief.
                                    –Lon Woodrum

Mary, "Whatever Jesus Says, Do It!"

Jesus and His disciples attended a wedding in Cana of Galilee. Jesus' mother was also there. There was not enough wine for the guests. Mary seemingly knew that Jesus possessed more than natural powers, for she told the servants, "Do whatever He tells you."

Jesus told them to fill six big stone water pots with water. They filled the pots to the brim, and at His word they served it. It was the choicest wine. This was Jesus' first public miracle.

Mary watched His ministry and His miracles. She treasured so many things about her dear son in her heart.

Mary, at the Cross

Mary stands by the cross of Jesus. (Only a mother's heart knows how dear and precious is her child.)

Mary has come to Jerusalem for the Passover. Instead of a time of remembrance and rejoicing in God's provision, she is watching with deep soul agony the crucifixion of her son. His torments are her tortures; her heart bleeds with His wounds. As her inward grief intensifies, the words "A sword shall pierce through your own soul," were fulfilled. Mary was cut to the heart. Tears coursed down her wrinkled cheeks. Scenes of His goodness, His kindness, and the many, many miracles He performed flash through her mind. As she shakes with sobs, she once again hears the voice of Jesus speaking to her tenderly, "Woman, behold thy son!"

Then to John, Jesus said, "Behold thy mother!" Even in dying, Jesus remembered His mother. He committed her to the trust-worthy keeping of John.

What a comfort for all who find true abundant life and peace in Jesus; but oh, how sad for those who reject Him. He is to them the Savior of death unto death.

At the Cross

Mary remembered the lowly manger,
The angelic announcement to the shepherds,
The brilliant glowing star,
The wise men's extravagant gifts from afar.
    At the cross.

Her mind traveled far that terrible day,
There at the cruel crucifixion,

Sobs wracked her slender frame,
Was it for this that Jesus came?
To die on a cross.

His torments were her torture,
Her heart bled with His wounds,
Yet somehow strength she found,
God's divine power did abound,
By His cross.

Now her son Jesus was dying,
A slow and pain-filled death,
This man who had made many whole,
A sword pierced His mother's soul,
At the cross.

Jesus looked down from the cross,
With eyes full of pity and love,
Woman, behold thy son,
Peace, no matter what man has done,
At the cross.

He said to John, "Behold thy mother."
John knew he meant, you care for her,
His mother was in His heart,
John provided for her and did his part,
After the cross.

MARY, IN THE MIDST OF BELIEVERS

The last time Mary is mentioned in Scripture is in Acts 1:14. "These all continued with one accord in prayer and supplication, with the women, and Mary the mother of Jesus, and with his brethren."

This happened just after Jesus' ascension. The believers are in the Upper Room, praying for the baptism of the Holy Ghost. Mary is with the disciples of Jesus, without any noticeable pre-eminence. Her risen Son is now her loving Savior.

PREGNANCY AND PRAISE

Mary and Elizabeth's example of spending much time with God and His Word before the birth of their sons is worthy of serious consideration. The unborn child is affected by his mother's affections, her moods, anxieties, and her joys!

My late mother-in-law, Elizabeth Beachy, related that when she was expecting her seventh child, her heart was filled with joy. She would sing and sing and sing as she went about her daily duties.

They were making changes in their lifestyle that gave them more input from the Word of God, and her heart was full of praise.

The child she carried grew to be one with a passion for godly music. As a youth, he would spend hours singing song after song in his room, till his mother would call up the steps, "Mark, it is time to go to bed!"

All that added up to be a bonus for me. One of the dreams of my youth was to marry a man who loved to sing.

Singing and studying the Word of God will bless your life at any time. When you are expecting a child, it will bless the tiny new spark of life within you. Pray for your unborn child. Read the Word of God aloud to him. A worthy goal during pregnancy is to start with Psalm 1, and read a Psalm aloud each day for yourself and your unborn child.

IN WHAT DO YOU DELIGHT?

Mary, the mother of Jesus, delighted in God. She loved His Word. She was sweetly submissive to His will. For our lives to honor God and to be a blessing, we must delight in God, in His Word, and in His will. To delight in something is to intensely desire it, to want it, to greatly value it. Experiencing delight is to have a high degree of pleasure, desire, and enjoyment. In what, and in whom, does my heart delight?

1. Delight in God, be a Lover of God!

"Delight thyself also in the Lord, and he shall give thee the desires of thy heart" (Psalm 37:4).

To delight in God, I must make sure my heart, my love, my all is His.

I love to talk with Mark. When he is extra busy and we hardly communicate, I feel lonely and somehow cheated. I don't like when I feel distant from him. I know that to have a good marriage, we must communicate.

In my walk with God, is that how it works? Do I delight to talk to God each morning, each day? Do I value time with God enough to get up early to seek Him and pray while the house is still quiet?

Every morning lean thine arms
Upon the windowsill of heaven,
Then with the vision in thy heart,
Turn strong to meet thy day.
                    –Author Unknown

Regardless of our age and stage in life, we all need more and more of God to be fulfilled. If you do not spend time with God each day, it is not because you are too busy, but because you do not care enough about God.

2. Delight in God's Word, be a Lover of God's Word!

"Blessed is the man… whose delight is in the law of the Lord, and in his law doth he meditate day and night" (Psalm 1:2).

David writes in Psalm 119, "Thy testimonies are my delight… I will delight myself in thy commandments which I have loved… I delight in thy law…thy law is my delight."

The greatest piece of literature in the world is the Bible: treasure it more highly than any other book.

Do you delight in God's Word enough that you want to read it each day? Reading God's Word daily is the best habit you can ever acquire!

Here are two rules that will help you to be self-disciplined:

Read when you feel like it; read when you don't.

No Bible, no breakfast. "I have esteemed the words of his mouth more than my necessary food" (Job 23:12).

Learn to delight in studying your Sunday school lessons. Find joy in making word studies from Scripture. Make a study from Proverbs about the importance of our speech. What does the Bible say about modesty? What does it say about children?

We can never exhaust the Word of God. Delight in learning more and more.

George Mueller remarked, "I believe the one chief reason that I have been kept in happy useful service is that I have been a lover of Holy Scripture. It has been my habit to read the Bible through 4 times a year, in a prayerful spirit, to apply it to my heart, and to practice what I find there. I have been for 69 years a happy man."

3. Delight in God's will, be sweetly submissive!

"I delight to do thy will, O my God" (Psalm 40:8).

Do I delight in the work God has given me to do?

A married woman with a family does not have to ponder, "What is God's will for me?"

In Proverbs 31, we are called to look well to the ways of our household; to work diligently with our hands as we bless our husband and children. Count it a privilege to be able to work! My daily responsibilities are God given. My work is a place where I can choose to surrender, obey, and please Him!

There are strange ways of serving God;
You sweep a room, or turn a sod,
And suddenly to your surprise,
You hear the whir of seraphim,
And find you're under God's own eye,
And building palaces for Him.

—Author Unknown

If you are a teacher, a nurse, a missionary, or a mother, whatever your occupation, give it your best. God can enable you to truly delight in the work He calls you to do.

Titus 2 says women should love their husband and their children. We need to take time to nurture our marriages and to love and delight in our children. They have a never-dying soul and are truly priceless. Make sure their days are filled with words of encouragement from you:

"Thanks for sweeping the basement so well."

"You did a great job of mowing the lawn."

"I greatly appreciated how you were kind to the neighbors' little girl when she visited."

"The bread you made was delicious; keep up the good work!"

Do things to make your children happy. Take time to read stories, play games, go on walks, work together. Will you regret it when your children are grown? Never!

Look for sunshine, the blessings in your days. Seek, find, and appreciate all the good. One evening my six-year-old thanked me for mending a hole in his socks. His words were a sunbeam to my heart. Another day, my little son and I went out to gather the eggs. Upon entering the chicken house he piped up, "Good morning, chickens," and when we walked out with his little basket full of fresh brown eggs, he sang out, "Thank you, chickens!"

God can help us delight in our work and in our homes. Delight in praying for your children, in playing with them, and in pointing them to God!

Goals for Godly Mothering

Ask yourself: what kind of mother does God want me to be? Sit down and write some goals. One Sunday in our Sunday school class, I was challenged when we ladies shared goals for mothering. We also discussed things we want our children to remember about us.

Goals for Mothers

1. I want to live out what I ask of my children: that nothing is too small to pray about. I want to help them to take their problems to God and pray about everything.

2. I want to make my home a haven of rest for my family.

3. I like to pray for each of my children as I iron their clothes.

4. I want to help my children enjoy work and let them see that it is fun to be a mother. I want to make motherhood appealing, so that someday they'll want to be a mother.

5. I want to teach manners and Biblical truths cheerfully, not just nag.

6. I want my children to be able to enjoy where we live and find rest and relaxation at home. I want them to like to bring their friends to our house. I want to enjoy life with them. That takes some organization.

7. I want our home to be happy. If it is, Christianity and the way I live out my faith can better appeal to my children.

8. I want to take time to give each child individual attention. Talk with them, share, and learn what their dreams are. I want to ask them, "What would you like to do when you grow up?"

9. I want to compliment them and not get upset when they break things. (I don't want things to be that dear to me.)

10. I want to make our home a place of good memories. I want to take time for my small children, like a picnic on the deck with my two-year-old. I want to take time to eat with them, not just quickly get my work done.

I want my children to be able to remember that I:

· took time for them, and didn't just work.

· loved their dad.

· was calm and happy.

· was a praying mom, and did not panic when things went wrong.

· sang as I worked in the kitchen.

My Missionary Mother

–Sharon Kuepfer

Clara Schnupp is given to supporting her husband Clair. The vision to reach the lost is a burning passion in her heart and in the heart of her husband. What a beautiful blessing when a husband and wife work together in service for the King. Their vision has also greatly impacted the lives of their children and grandchildren.

Last evening, I held my weekly Bible study in the jail. Five lady inmates attended. A first-time offender. A Philippine lady. Others. They sat still, eyes fixed on me, waiting, yearning for some sort of hope for their troubled lives.

Holding my Bible on my lap, I looked into their eyes and read aloud two verses that had blessed me that morning. We sang. Soon it was time to go. I prayed for them and left some New Testaments with those who had none.

I drove home to my loyal husband and precious children, reflecting on those dear women. Many of the women I meet in prison seem to have no chance. The beatings, the abuse, the broken homes; at times it seems beyond comprehension.

My thoughts wandered to my mother. As a nine-year-old child of Russian Mennonite immigrants, she lived on the prairies of Manitoba. There, she embraced her missionary call. That call has never left her—I suppose it never will. Because she believes in the One who called her, I have never heard my mother say, "This is such a hopeless situation," or "There's no help for that person."

About three quarters of the year, Dad and Mom are away from home on missionary travels, meeting many people in desperate situations. Years ago, when Dad asked her to marry him, he also inquired if she would be willing to go anywhere in the world with him. She was deeply in love. She said, "Of course, Dear." Little did she know that her commitment would indeed take her all over the globe as she journeyed with Dad, telling about God's great love that gives hope in the face of hopelessness.

Recently, Mom went on a walk with my friend and me. My mother has learned that exercise helps to control her diabetes. As we stepped along, my mother related stories of her walks on missionary trips. "I know many villages through and through," she commented.

She chattered on to my friend and me about a walking escapade in Greenland. Because she wanted an item from their mission plane, she informed Dad, "I'll just walk out to the airport and get it."

"It's a long way," he remarked.

She didn't mind, and she headed out the door. After walking awhile, she spied some ladies visiting at a picnic table by the side of the road.

They yelled to her, "Where are you going?"

Eyeing their beer bottles sitting on the table, Mom warily replied, "To the airport."

"We'll call a taxi for you, but we want to talk to you when you return."

Sure enough, a taxi soon arrived. After completing her errand at the plane, Mom asked the taxi man to drop her off close to the ladies. He gave her a surprised glance, but did as she asked.

She approached the women. Having had a bit of the strong stuff, they were rather talkative. Having seen and heard the worst that life can bring, she fearlessly sat down.

"What are you doing here?" one woman wondered.

Mom replied, "My husband and I are here to help people learn to take the pain of their hearts to Jesus."

Wanting to be hospitable, the women offered her some beer.

"No thanks," she answered.

"Tea?" one of them asked.

"Sure."

"But we don't have a clean cup," continued the generous lady.

"Oh, I'll just rinse mine out with beer."

Although I'm not sure I could have stomached the stuff or the cup, my mother calmly drank the strangest, most unique tea she had ever sipped.

The ladies began sharing their many problems. I can picture Mom sitting and listening, but also sharing about Jesus' love, because she's not afraid to go to the heart of the matter. I can also picture her praying with those derelicts of society.

As we strolled along, Mom told us yet another "walking" story. This time, she was swinging along, singing as she went, in a town on the Canadian tundra.

A lady stopped her, and asked, "Why are you singing?"

Mom replied, "I sing to God and thank Him for things and worship Him."

The lady then shared her struggles with Mom. She cried. Then they prayed together.

After hearing these stories, my friend started sharing some of her problems. (It was as though she thought, *If others share with Clara, I might as well take advantage of it, too!*) I was glad Mom was there—people seem to take her advice to heart. In comparison, I feel like a child yet, attempting to learn. Mom listened, asked questions, gave a bit of wisdom, and then and there, she prayed.

Next, she suggested, "Get others to pray for you. Don't just say, 'Pray for me,' and leave. Allow them to pray for you right away."

I grew up hearing Mom frequently quote Matthew 18:20. "For where two or three are gathered together in my name, there am I in the midst of them." When I was sixteen, I wrote the following poem about my mother's prayers:

My Prayer Warrior

She doesn't just fight when the battles are raging
Nor when the tempest is over.
She doesn't spend long hours in the center of the battle
Where spectators can watch with awe.
But she gets the work done at the sides…
Quietly…
    Slowly…
        But that's where the victory is won.

Mom has more stories. Her storytelling (of their missionary trips) continually influences others around her. Recently my children and I sat enthralled while she related the following story:

She and Dad had been in a North American city teaching Bible lessons. One of the women in the class approached Mom and said, "Some of us discussed you and Clair, and your amazing energy. How do you do it? You hear so many awful stories of abuse, neglect, and violence. How can you keep going?"

As we gathered around her, Mom told us her answer: "After we hear so many stories, we realize that none are new. The themes remain consistent—the hurt, the pain, the sin. But God's answers are the same, too." Mom never seems to tire of counseling others to forgive and to grasp God's hand of forgiveness.

At that same seminar, Mom sat in the back of the room while Dad shared Bible teachings with a small group. Sometimes Dad will ask Mom to comment. Her affirmations sometimes speak louder than the concepts Dad teaches, because her life testifies to what he preaches.

The attendees included some long-time Christians, and also non-Christians. Suddenly, a slightly intoxicated man shuffled in the door and toward the front where Dad was speaking. He had been attending the earlier sessions, and Dad and Mom were puzzled why he hadn't returned.

He took the microphone from Dad and said, "I was sexually abused by a minister when I was young. When you were talking about forgiving sexual abusers, I got angry, and walked out to drink. I just wanted to say that I will try to come back tomorrow."

While this admission was probably healthy, Dad knew that the drunk man, in his present state of mind, might keep interrupting the sessions. Dad motioned Mom off to the side, and asked her, "Can you take him out of the room and talk to him?" Calmly, my mother did just that. Mom led Ben, the alcohol-reeking man, out of the room. She and Ben then saw his girlfriend, who was also intoxicated and started crying on Ben's shoulder. Mom asked, "Why are you crying?"

She sobbed, "My daughter committed suicide." Finally, after sharing her troubles with Mom for awhile, the girlfriend told Ben, "I am leaving."

Brusquely he replied, "Go ahead."

The girlfriend left. For the next two hours, Ben talked and cried. Once again, it was easy to picture my mother comforting him and listening to him, as if he were the son she never had. Mom believes with all her heart that nothing is too big for God.

Ben's story was heartbreaking. His troubles began when he was young. His minister abused him. He ran home and told his mother. She slapped him. "You are lying," she announced. His grandma said Jesus would punish him for saying such bad things about the minister.

The biggest thing that came to the surface was that Ben felt the abuse was his fault. Because he was hungry, he had asked the minister for two dollars. By this time in the discussion, his mind was clearing a bit. Mom said, "Ben, there was nothing wrong with a hungry boy asking for money." When she said that, he cried like a baby. She sat with him as his heart turned tender.

Mom asked, "Why don't you come and have breakfast with my husband in the morning at 7:00?" Considering the condition of his mind and body, she figured that he would have to be very serious about getting help if he would make it that early.

Guess what? Ben showed up at ten minutes to seven the next morning! For an hour and a half, Dad and Mom took him through the three basic longings of the heart: we all need to feel accepted, we all are worth something, and we can do things successfully. Dad moved on to help him define his feelings. They encouraged him to uncover the lies that he believed about himself and the vows he made to try to make life work without God. He saw how he was living out his life, distancing himself with walls, violence, and anger.

Mom told us, "He really seemed to get the picture." He then took the pen out of Dad's hand, turned the page over, and wrote: "And then all the people I have hurt." In such a short time he was seeing the need to take responsibility for his own sins, and to ask others to forgive him. His life had been a mess of sin and sorrow. He has been in and out of penitentiary three times. To top it all off, his son was killed on the railroad a few months before.

After their breakfast, Ben attended Clair Schnupp's seminar. At the late afternoon service, Ben gave his story. He really had understood the need to forgive.

"He was close to the kingdom," Mom told us. "We are praying for him. There are Christians in his community." This is what Mom often falls back on—the local church to pick up where she and Dad have left off. The brotherhood and God need to do the rest.

I ponder my mother's life. Wherever God calls me, I want to model her by "being there." Numbers don't matter to her. God has simply asked her to go with her husband. She is not afraid to enter into the middle of the chaos of people's unlovable lives.

My mom has chosen a self-sacrificing way of life. She belongs to the King. She fulfills her duties with a joy that really can't come from anywhere on earth.

I want to open up myself to God as my mother does, so that all whom I minister to can know they're not seeing me, but Christ. And when they see Christ, they'll know the God who loves to do the impossible—the God of my missionary mother.

CHAPTER THREE

Praise, Prayer, and Senior Years

The life of Anna testifies to the truth of Psalm 92:12-15: "The righteous shall flourish like the palm tree: he shall grow like a cedar in Lebanon. Those that be planted in the house of the Lord shall flourish in the courts of our God. They shall still bring forth fruit in old age; they shall be fat and flourishing; to show that the Lord is upright; he is my rock, and there is no unrighteousness in him."

She was old. But she was not old and bitter. She was not old and full of complaints. Rather, Anna was full of thankfulness and praising the Lord.

She lived up to the delightful meaning of her name. Anna: one who is kind, benevolent, desiring to do good to others, merciful, and compassionate.

There are three verses in the Bible about Anna (Luke 2:36-38). We read that Anna was a prophetess, a widow whose husband died after only seven years of marriage, and she was "of great age."

She loved God so much that she did not depart from the temple; it could be she lived in a room of the temple courts, or she was always there whenever the doors were opened.

One day, her faithful attendance and devotion were rewarded. She arrived at exactly the right moment. Joseph and Mary had come to the temple to present their infant Jesus to the Lord. Simeon was holding the precious babe in his arms and blessing God.

Anna saw this sacred scene, she heard Simeon's words, and likewise gave thanks to the Lord. She was certain that this child was the promised Messiah, the desire of all ages. The hope of a long lifetime was fulfilled in this brief encounter.

Because Simeon and Anna were so in tune with God, they recognized the baby Jesus as the true Messiah!

What a blessing it was to these three generations, the aged and the young parents with the baby Jesus, to worship God together. Each heart was aflame with love for God. Joseph and Mary were amazed and encouraged at the words which were spoken of their child. Mary wondered how a sword would someday pierce her own soul. Years later at the awful crucifixion of her Son, she would understand.

Anna, the prophetess, had understanding in the Scriptures. She made it her business to instruct others in the things of God. Anna's purpose was to share God's Word. She knew where to find those who believed the Scriptures and looked for the promised Messiah. She told them all the good news of how she had seen the infant Lord Jesus.

Anna, a devout woman of prayer and perseverance, loved God with all her heart. While others ate, drank, or slept, she was pouring out her devotion to God by fasting and praying, night and day.

Agonizing in prayer takes great energy. It is the most valuable work in the kingdom. It is a work that age cannot rob us of. Whatever your age, prayer is a ministry and a mission for all of God's children.

Because she was filled with God and His Word, Anna became a woman of praise. She was a woman prepared to serve God, and prepared to die. Her heart was so focused on God that, in spite of old age and widowhood, she gave thanks.

Anna is remembered for her praise, her prayers, and her dedication to God. If three verses were written about your life, what would they say?

MAKE MY DAY

Is there anything we can do to bless the lives of the elderly people among us?

I talked with Anna Mullet, a senior from our church, on the street of our little town of Sugarcreek. She told me she met our children on the sidewalk, and they all said "Hi" to her. "Some folks don't bother saying hello to an old woman like me," she remarked. "Just saying, 'Hi, how are you?' can make my day."

Lizzie, one of my elderly friends, related, "A dear teenage girl stops in at our house occasionally. She tells us what is happening in her world. What a wonderful way to brighten our day!" Lizzie also appreciates a young Sunday school teacher who comes to class loaded with interesting information. She remembers what she studied!

Senor citizens are blessed when youth take time to talk to them at church. They are encouraged when they see youth living for God, and perceive in them the fruits of obedience, honesty, and truthfulness.

God calls us to serve Him in many different ways. For some elderly, their first priority must be to care for an ailing partner. That can be a difficult, demanding service to offer up to God. As time and health allow, others enjoy volunteer work. Still others use their gift of encouragement by sharing kind words, or by sending a cheery note, card, or letter.

CHALLENGES OF AGING

At times when our house is full of lively, noisy children, and there is much work to be done, I wistfully think of retirement and a slower pace. Our mealtimes are full of chatter. Some of our table times are too loud and noisy. Mark and I can hardly speak to one another.

My friend, who has an empty nest, says, "Enjoy these days; they are the best. When our children left, it was so quiet we could hear each other chew at mealtimes. That was not fun."

The idea of growing old does not appeal to many people. The decline of health certainly is not easy. Loss of hearing, forgetfulness, and absentmindedness are not desirable.

One lady related that she was preparing a meal, and was searching high and low for her frying pan. Finally, she found it. The pan was on her stove, and the fish were already frying in it!

To no longer have the strength to do all their own work is difficult for the elderly. Accepting help is humbling. Most everyone would rather be able to do their own work.

We wonder why some people are blessed with a sound mind and good health. Others struggle year in and year out with Alzheimer's, Parkinson's disease, dementia, open-heart surgery, or cancer.

Matthew Henry writes in his commentary, "Nothing is more likely to ruffle the thoughts and put the body into disorder than acute pain and distemper of the body."

It behooves us to be compassionate and caring to those who are suffering the trials of aging.

Only God knows the "why" of the many puzzling questions in life. We can rest in the fact that God is always with us; He always cares. We can learn from the example of Job. His trials were most severe, and his pain was extreme. Yet Job did not give up his faith in God. He said, "Though he slay me, yet will I trust in him" (Job 13:15).

Blessings in Growing Old

Are there any positive aspects of growing old? "Yes, indeed," I am told. "One of the best things is grandchildren, and even great-grandchildren! Grandchildren give you another opportunity to influence a child for God.

The apostle Timothy's grandmother influenced him for the Lord. Think! What can you as a grandmother do to make your faith personal and attractive to the next generation?

My friend Alice said that when their grandsons come to visit, they require them to spend some time quietly reading in the evening. They have interesting, character-building books for them to read. One evening, her grandson was quiet for so long that she got worried. She was grateful when she realized that he enjoyed the book so much that he was still reading.

Mary Ann says she likes to sing "Jesus Loves Me" to her grand-daughter. Erinna must feel special, for Mary Ann also sings "You Are My Sunshine." She likes to call the grandchildren who live hundreds of miles away. She sends them postcards to brighten their days.

Grandchildren give you a fresh perspective on life. Enjoy the beauties of nature and play together.

When you retire, there is time to do crafts. There is plenty of quiet time to read and meditate. You have learned to be more pa-tient and kind, more tolerant of others, and the little aggravations of life are no longer so aggravating.

The enemy of our souls wants grandparents to feel useless; yet, as long as you live, there is still the opportunity to witness and reach out to others. Pray, and pray some more. After all, praying for your grandchildren is one of the most important things you can do for them!

Though our society fears aging, God's children have nothing to fear. We can look forward to a deepening walk with God in our old age, and trust that He will provide. Best of all is the wonderful anticipation that each day we are moving closer to our departure, or the Lord's return!

Hold on to Faith!
When death stared Paul
Full in the face,
With confidence he said,
"I have kept the faith!"

Thirty Thousand Nights

Today, there are still elderly women who are totally given to God. Their lives are a shining beacon, proclaiming the victory and peace for those who trust, love, and serve God every day. Barbara Barnheart is like Anna: faithful and flourishing for Jesus in her senior years.

Life has not been all roses for Barbara, who has been a widow for over thirty years. Her goal is to reach that heavenly home where "the roses never fade."

Barbara was thirty-six when she married Jim. God gave them three lovely children and nearly fifteen years together. Jim's last two years were fraught with pain and fighting cancer. Their youngest daughter was extra close to her daddy. Years later, she told her mom how hard it was for her. She couldn't understand why a God of love would cause her daddy to suffer (she saw him suffer intensely), and then have her grow up without a daddy. Somehow, they made it through those dark, difficult days.

Barbara continues to pray daily for her children. Decisions made by some of them have caused her grief. "The Lord was there for me," Barbara confided. When he was eighteen, her son enlisted in the army without discussing it with her or any other Christian.

"I felt the Lord prompting me to tell my son, 'No matter where you go, or what you do, my love will ALWAYS be there for you.'" She kept up communication with him the four years he was gone, including one year in Korea. He became involved in drugs, alcohol, and smoking.

Today, Barbara rejoices that he has been free of all those things for a number of years now. She continues to pray each day that her children and their families would experience the Lord in their lives before it is too late.

"Before I go to sleep at night I rest in the promise, 'The angel of the Lord encampeth round about them that fear him, and delivereth them.' God has watched over me now for thirty thousand nights. Praise His name," testifies Barbara.

"I am thoroughly enjoying my senior years," Barbara shared. "I am continuing to rejoice in the Lord. He is the only REAL source of joy and peace. He is so faithful. The Lord has blessed me super abundantly with energy and health for my age. He has also provided ways of ministering."

The ministry of cleaning: Barbara cleans eight different houses for elderly people who are not physically able. Each one of the folks she cleans for are good friends. She has cleaned some of the houses for more than fifteen years. One of the ladies she cleans for is in her nineties. She told Barbara, "I tell folks I have a friend who cleans for me. I don't call you my cleaning lady."

"Dr. Martin Luther King said: 'If a man is called to be a street sweeper, he should sweep streets even as Michelangelo painted, or Beethoven composed music, or Shakespeare composed poetry. He should sweep streets so well that all the hosts of heaven and earth will pause to say, "Here lived a great street sweeper, who did his job well."'"[2]

Ministry of Gardening: Barbara's daughter Alma and her family lived in Brooklyn, New York, for many years. Barbara rejoices greatly that Alma is a dedicated, godly wife and mother, and an influence in their New York community. She supports their ministry by raising and canning green beans, at least eighty quarts. God blesses her tomatoes, and she cans tomato juice, pizza sauce, and more for them.

Keeping busy and active promotes good health and well-being. The gardener is in partnership with God. You pray, sow, water, and weed. God sends the sunshine, the rain, and the harvest.

My mother taught me this lovely poem:

Out in the Fields with God
The little cares that fretted me, I lost them yesterday,
Among the fields, above the sea, among the winds at play,
Among the lowing of the herds, the rustling of the trees,
Among the singing of the birds, the humming of the bees.

The fears of what may come to pass, I cast them all away,
Among the clover-scented grass, among the new-mown hay,
Among the rustling of the corn, where drowsy posies nod,
Where ill thoughts die and good are born, out in the fields
with God.

—Louise Imogen Guiney

Ministry of prayer: Barbara regularly prays for her ministers and teachers in their church school. "Some of these men I cuddled as babies. Now they minister to me as pastors, choristers, and superintendents. I love to express my appreciation to them," she says.

In 1909, Jonathan Goforth, missionary to China, was visiting friends in London. He was taken to visit an invalid, who told him she had sensed a great burden laid upon her to pray for Goforth. She had heard of his plans for meetings in Manchuria, and beseeched heaven's throne to bless Goforth's ministry. She recorded three dates when she sensed a special power in prayer.

Jonathan recalled those dates as the very days when he had witnessed God mightily at work.[3]

"How little they know who languish in what seems useless sickrooms, amid restrictions of frail health, what work they do for Christ by the power of saintly living and by even fragmentary prayers."[4]

Truly, we are laborers together with God.

Ministry of sewing: Barbara's friends give her scrap materials, which she cuts into neat squares and then sews them together for warm comfort tops. Her church has a sewing circle day. They knot the comforts, and quilt lovely quilts for the needy.

My mother and Aunt Lydia work on similar projects. Aunt Lydia said, "It may seem like a lowly thing, but we do it for the glory of God, and it gives us satisfaction to go on doing it." My aunt also said, "We like to sing the song, 'Ready to go, ready to stay, ready my place to fill, ready for service, lowly or great, ready to do His will.'"

How beautiful the faith and confidence of those who are ready to live or ready to die for God.

Ministry of Christian schools: Years ago, Barbara taught school. She is still excited about their school. Monday mornings, she has a merit shop for grades two to twelve at her church's Christian Day School. She washes the cleaning rags each week, a responsibility she has fulfilled for twenty-five years. She enjoys anything involving the school. She finds fulfillment in relating to children.

I think Barbara would tell us:

Look at the small hands of a child. They are the hands of the future.

Those hands may someday either:

Hold a Bible… or else a deadly weapon

Lead in church singing… or spin a gambling wheel

Dress a wound as a nurse… or tremble because they are controlled by alcohol…

Blessed are those who influence children for God!

· ·

"Thou shalt rise up before the hoary head, and honor the face of the old man, and fear thy God: I am the Lord" (Leviticus 19:32).

· ·

The most often repeated commandment in the Bible is "Fear not." Remember that when you dread another birthday.

· ·

"For this God is our God forever and ever: he will be our guide even unto death" (Psalm 48:14).

· ·

"And even to your old age I am he; and even to hoar hairs will I carry you; I have made, and I will bear; even I will carry, and will deliver you" (Isaiah 46:4).

· ·

The ability to replace complaining with praising is the secret to growing old well.

· ·

When you were born, you cried, and the world rejoiced. Live so that when you die, the world cries, and you rejoice!

· ·

"How far you go in life depends on your being tender with the young, compassionate with the aged, sympathetic with the striving, and tolerant of the weak and the strong, because someday you will have been all of these."

−George Washington Carver

CHAPTER FOUR

The Unnamed Woman

Devotion is defined as an earnest attachment to a cause or a person, it is the ready will to *serve* God. In this story we see one woman's devotion to Jesus. A devotion that reminds me of King David's words, "Neither will I offer burnt offerings to the Lord my God of that which doth cost me nothing" (II Samuel 24:24).

Imagine the scene: it is only a few days before the crucifixion. Jesus and His disciples are feasting at the house of a man known as Simon the leper. Simon had likely been healed of this terrible disease by Jesus, and his deep gratitude is expressed by preparing this feast (Matthew 26:6-13).

This was a feast for men. In Jewish culture, women undoubtedly kept to the background. A Jewish prayer contained this line, "Blessed be God who did not make me a woman." It was, they thought, a mark of piety not to speak to any woman. No man would speak to a woman he did not know.

Now, enter a woman. She comes to Jesus, close to Him. Quite likely, the men feel she came brazenly. She breaks her alabaster flask and pours precious, expensive ointment on the head of Jesus. The room is filled with a lovely fragrance. Jesus knows this is an act of supreme love and respect.

In those days, it was a common courtesy to pour a bit of

perfume on arriving guests. Perfume was also used to anoint a body for burial. But this was not the duty of this woman. The disciples were not impressed; rather, they were deeply disgusted. "Why such a waste?" they mutter. "You could have sold that ointment for much, and helped the poor."

It would seem that Jesus sighed. "Why do you trouble and criticize the woman?" He responds. "She has done a beautiful thing, a good work. You will always have the poor with you, but you won't always have me. She did it for my burial."

What a sad state it was for the disciples to find fault with the woman's devotion.

Did this woman understand Jesus' frequent predictions of His death and suffering better than His disciples did? Perhaps her womanly intuition sensed the tragedy ahead. The oil she poured on Jesus' head was a lavish gesture of affection—a bright star of love and loyalty against all the dark background of hatred, deception, and treachery that Jesus would experience in the coming days.

Jesus gave an astounding testimony of honor and recognition to the deed of this woman. "She hath done what she could. She came early to anoint my body for burial. Throughout the whole world, wherever the gospel is preached, this shall be spoken of for a memorial of her."

The Lord God of Israel said, "Them that honor me I will honor" (I Samuel 2:30). "She hath done what she could." Could those same words be spoken of you and me?

Our lives will leave a mark for eternity. What record will you and I leave? When God calls us home, what will we be remembered by?

Remembered by What?

Oh my God, when my time will come to die,
What will my hands be remembered by?

Had I reached out to the needy with love?
Deeds remembered by my Father above.

Did I care when someone was lonely or sad?
Took time for a call to make them glad?

Had I time to lift my hands in prayer?
My home; the beauty of Jesus, was it there?

Were my hands extended with kindness and love?
To visit the sick, honoring God above?

Oh my God, when my time shall come to die,
What will my hands be remembered by?

My Gifts to Jesus

Is our love and devotion for Jesus of such depth that we could say, "Nothing is too good for Him. Nothing is so precious that it should be withheld from Jesus"?

Matthew 2:11 says the wise men searched for and found Jesus. They bowed down and worshiped Him. They opened their treasures, and presented unto Him gifts: gold, frankincense, and myrrh.

What do we as women have to give our Lord?
What does He yearn for and desire from us?
What is most precious to us?

My gold to give to Jesus is my heart, my husband, and my children.

Gold is costly. In II Samuel 24:24 David said, "Shall I give to God that which cost me nothing?"

My heart: Jesus wants my ALL, my heart's deepest love and devotion.

Can I echo the deep words of devotion from the hymn "Lord Send Me Anywhere"?

Lord, send me anywhere, only go with me,

Lay any burden on me, only sustain me,
Sever any tie, save the tie that binds me to thy heart,
Lord Jesus, my King, I consecrate my life, Lord, to Thee.

My husband: I release him to the Lord. I want to be willing to give my husband to God and His work. I need to beware of controlling him. I need to guard against resenting his schedule.

I want to desire most of all that he would be a man totally sold out for God. It is worth it to yield all to God.

In the garden of Eden, there was no frustration of wishing for more time together. That paradise was lost with the fall of man. Since then, women have struggled with longing for more time with their husbands. Maybe that desire is also a longing for more of God, a longing for our eternal home, and a call to seek Him more fervently.

My children: I give them to God.

What are my goals for them? Is it that they would stay nearby and bless me, or do I desire most of all that they would grow to be children of God and workers for Him wherever He leads them?

In I Samuel 1, we read how Hannah longed for a son. She vowed that if God gave her a son, she would give him to the Lord all the days of his life. When her desire was granted, she loved her son. I believe she did all she could to influence and touch his heart for God in the few short years he was sheltered under her love. Then she fulfilled her vow, and took him to Eli to serve God in the temple. Hannah said, "I have lent him to the Lord; as long as he liveth he shall be lent to the Lord."

I am challenged by the example of Amy Carmichael's mother. Before Amy went to India, Amy asked her, "My precious mother, have you given me unreservedly to the Lord for whatever He wills? May He strengthen you to say yes to Him, if He asks you something that costs."

Her mother's response is simply beautiful.

"Amy, He is yours, you are His to take you where He pleases, to use you as He wills. I can trust you to Him, and I do. All day long He has helped me, and my heart unfailingly says 'go ye.'"[5]

Amy went to India. She was useful, faithful, and fruitful in the work of God.

"Oh Lord, I give You my gold—my heart, my husband, my children."

My frankincense to give are my prayers and my praise.

Frankincense, an ingredient in the perfume that was burned in a dish in the most holy part of the temple, filled the air with royal fragrance. Revelation 5:8 says, "The four and twenty elders fell down before the Lamb, having every one of them harps, and golden vials full of odors, which are the prayers of the saints."

God loves to hear His children praying. Offer daily your gift of prayer. Prayer for your children is a gift that cannot be measured.

Mother's Covers
When you were small
And just a touch away,
I covered you with blankets
Against the cool night air
But now that you are tall
And out of reach,
I fold my hands
And cover you with prayer.
                    –Unknown

Praying and singing helps us to focus our minds on God. God loves to hear His children singing. David said in Psalm 27:6, …"therefore will I offer in his tabernacle sacrifices of joy; I will sing, yea, I will sing praises unto the Lord."

I recall one December when my baby had ear infections and was fussy. He had many restless nights. I was tired and dreaded all the extra activities of the month. I needed to go to God, implore His help, and praise Him. Prayer and praise gives strength to cope through difficult days of mothering small children. Philippians 4:6-7 encourages us to pray about everything. God's peace will keep our hearts and minds.

My frankincense to give is my prayers and praise.

My myrrh to give is a life of "yes" to God and "no" to self.

Myrrh was used as a spice or medicine; it was also used in embalming. Myrrh is a symbol of being yielded to God, saying "yes" to His will and "no" to myself. Psalm 51:17: "The sacrifices of God are a broken spirit: a broken and a contrite heart, O God, thou wilt not despise."

I want to grow in trusting God through the unplanned and hard things of life; an unexpected pregnancy, the loss through a miscarriage, the death of a dream. So many things in life are beyond my control, but God is in control. Saying "yes" pleases Him.

At times, I have a problem with saying "yes" in the small things of ordinary days. One Saturday morning, I longed to sleep a little longer, at least till 7:00. Shouldn't boys sleep longer on a Saturday morning? Two of the boys woke before 6:30. Soon another little son was awake. Instead of welcoming them all with warm, loving arms, I had a bad attitude. I set Micah on the floor, left them all in Mark's care, and stomped to the bathroom to wash my hair.

Proverbs 16:3 says, "Commit thy works unto the Lord, and thy thoughts shall be established." When I verbally give each day to God, even before I get out of bed, I can cope better with what the day holds. "Yes," Lord. "Yes" to motherhood. "Yes" to caring for boys. "Yes" to choosing to be a joyful mother!

When Mary was told she was chosen to be the mother of Jesus, she said, "Behold the handmaid of the Lord; be it unto me according to thy word" (Luke 1:38). What an example of submission to strive to follow.

My myrrh to give is "YES" to God and "no" to self.

Elizabeth Elliot said, "The Father pours out His blessings on us; we His creatures receive them with open hands, give thanks, and lift them up as an offering back to Him, thus completing the circle."

All that we are, all that we have is a gift from God. Ultimately, we are His! May we hold on to trust, faith, and devotion through all of life. Whether we are married or single, we need the Lord most of all!

Today, Jesus is calling each one of us to follow Him. He is calling us to minister and to serve. He is more among us than we realize. What we do for others, we do for Him.

DELIGHTING IN GOD'S CALLING WHETHER SINGLE OR MARRIED

Can I honestly say that Jesus is my all in all? I am not depending on marriage for my joy. I am not depending on a new house, a promotion, riches, or whatever it is I may desire. I am depending on Jesus!

Why do some lovely women never marry? Why do some married women never conceive? Why do some women suffer from so many illnesses? When we surrender to the sovereignty of God, we find peace in the things we don't understand in life. God is sovereign. Let God be God. I love the two little words, "God's will." Those two little words solve many questions. I find rest when I believe the will of God is good, acceptable, and perfect for me!

My heart is at rest when I know and embrace one theological truth: "My times are in God's hands." Embracing this truth will determine if my life and heart are filled with peace or panic.

It is interesting that we all, whether married or single, need the same basic things for joy and fulfillment in life. We need God, meaningful work, a heart of love and care, a servant's heart, and a prayer of "taking it all to God."

I would like to share six points that all queens of character (God's women) have, and five questions I asked numerous friends who are single.

1. A queen of character recognizes and surrenders to the sovereignty of God! She embraces the promise of Jeremiah 29:11, "For I know the plans I have for you," says the Lord. "They are plans for good and not evil, to give you a future and a hope."

"Why are you single?" (I asked this question of several single friends. Here are their answers.)

· God chose this life for me.

· It's not my choice, but God's. Because of that, I delight in Him, and attempt with His help to live a fulfilled life.

· The right one hasn't asked yet. (Sometimes I am tempted to feel I am single because I am inferior.)

· Everyone expects you to get married someday. If it doesn't happen, singles are left to feel it's their fault because they are too loud, bossy, shy, overweight, etc. Look at the married women; there are many that fit into that category. I do not believe it is fair (in most cases) to say she is not married because of a weakness in her life. She is single, because the Lord called her to be single for whatever reason He chose.

· No one that I wanted to marry ever asked me, and our cultural mores prevented me from asking him. The way I relate to men impacts my choice to remain single. My motivation, purpose, and identity in life do not revolve around marriage and having a family, though I am not opposed to such.

· At this point, it is my choice. We singles could all be married by lowering our standards or being aggressive with men. There are lots of men out in the world that would jump for a chance to be married to a Mennonite girl. Years ago, I could have lowered my standards. But where would I be? Marriage is not the ultimate. A relationship with my Lord is. I want to serve Him wherever He chooses.

2. Queens of character delight in God and know their relationship with Him is MOST important. They have meaningful work.

I Chronicles 16:11: "Seek the Lord and his strength, seek his face continually."

"What do you need to be fulfilled in life?"

· A walk with God, a relationship with Him. (This is paramount to happiness and fulfillment in life.)

· I need friends and children (such as teaching school).

· I need a servant's heart and a job I enjoy.

· I need the assurance that what I do is God's will, and contentment in that perfect will.

· Lucy Martin said, "I am happiest when I am extending myself for the good of others. I love to be busy. My interests range widely: I enjoy writing, art, gardening and cooking, needlework, crafts, and much more. I involve myself fully and wholly in my teaching career, and delight in seeing my students happy and successful, and their parents happy too. I am interested in each student as a person.

· Silvia Tarniceriu was once asked, "Are you glad you didn't get married in Romania long ago?" She responded, "Oh, yes, I am so busy. If I were married, I don't know what I would do with him. I could use him for my landscaping, but he might be too busy for that."

Silvia wonders why some singles have a sour face because they didn't marry. "Come on," she says. "There is work to do for the Lord. I didn't have time to pity myself that I wasn't married, and suddenly, I was fifty! My friend Elena got married, and that is fine for her. I AM HAPPY!"

Years ago, when Silvia was approached about having a book written about her life, she said to Harvey Yoder, "If you can write the book so people can remember my God, write it. If it is only so they can remember Silvia, don't write it."

Since the book was published, she has received many phone calls telling how *God Knows My Size* has been such a blessing and help.

I love Silvia's example of joyfulness and fulfillment in God's work. Serving God is her passion. Her joy in God is real, even though eight years ago she was diagnosed with breast cancer.

"There is no life without trials," Silvia shares. "It's not an easy road, but God is with me. He sees me through. Whatever you face today, remember, "God knows!"

3. Queens of character take an interest in others' lives. They work at being caring and friendly.

Teresa shared how two friends bless her. "They want my friendship, even if I am single. They take a deep interest in my life, including me in their family and family activities. They are always eager to talk with me, and find out what my week was like. They make me feel valuable and affirmed.

Lucy Martin said, "The nicest thing a married person (a student's parents) ever told me was, 'I hope she never gets married.' That told me that I am where I belong, and am needed here."

Lucy also said, "To my surprise, my married friends tell me how much I mean to them; then I tell them how much they mean to me. They act delighted to see me, and I am mutually delighted to see them."

Thanksgiving was just past when Mark's Aunt Anna Mae called. I always enjoy visiting with her. I asked her what she did on Thanksgiving Day. She replied, "I was at home, all alone. I don't think I should disturb family get-togethers!"

I felt badly. Surely Anna Mae's nieces and nephews should remember and include her over the holidays! That includes us. Anna Mae is in her seventies and lives alone. For many years, she cared for her parents. After God called them home she was the caretaker for her sister. She has been faithful. Now, what will we do to brighten her days?

There is a blessing in including singles in Sunday dinner invitations and other activities. When someone lives alone, it can give them a huge lift when a man offers to fix things for them.

"How do singles like married folks to relate to them, or how can your married friends bless you?"

· Accept me as a normal person, as worthy of your time as any person, tell me about your life, and vice versa.

- Take an interest in my life, job, hobbies. Don't just talk about yours.
- Treat me as a mature adult.
- Surprise me with a phone call; remember my birthday.
- Share, talk, listen.

4. Queens of character have a servant's heart.

Our goal is to be like Jesus. "For even the Son of man came not to be ministered unto, but to minister, and to give his life a ransom for many" (Mark 10:45).

Look at your surroundings. How could God use you? Why did God put you in the place you are? Pray, "Lord, what do you want me to do? Please give me inspiration on ways to bless others."

Some women are called to care for elderly parents. Others serve God for years and years on the mission field. Others bless the Lord by working at Penn Valley, Wildernessway Camp in South Carolina, an orphanage in Romania, and so much more!

One group of singles from Pennsylvania prepares a meal for the 12 widows in their church every month. They eat with them, or invite them to their own house.

Alta Beiler said she e-mails missionaries each week with church news: announcements, prayer requests, new babies, hospitalizations, tidbits from our services, weddings, engagements, youth activities, and whatever other news from home she thinks they would love to hear. She also sends baby congratulation cards to new parents and visits them.

There can be a real ministry with children for single women. You can touch a heart for God when you reach out to a child. It is important to build relationships with children!

Alta attempts to show special interest in the children at her church. "A couple from our church was visiting missionaries in Kenya. They went shopping in the markets. The mother asked her five-year-old son if he would like to buy some carved wooden animals to take home for his friends."

She asked him, "Who are your friends?" The first name he mentioned was Alta. When they returned from Kenya, she was the first person to receive a wooden animal. What a reward that was!

Consider baby-sitting a ministry. You minister to the couple, their children, and your community in that caring gesture of baby-sitting.

Once, when Rosanna baby-sat for us, she put a sign outside the front window that said, "Free cones!" She opened the window and handed the cones out to the delighted children drive-through style. We came home to happy children and a tidy house. We were blessed!

Gal. 6:10 reminds us that when we have opportunity, we should do good to all men, especially to those who are of the household of faith. I don't know what blesses parents as much as when someone befriends and is kind to their children.

My single friends have been such a blessing by their willingness to teach Sunday school and Bible school. They encourage our children to study their lessons, teach enthusiastically, and take time to befriend our children after church.

I thank God for Anna Marie, Miriam, and Ruth. They put their heart and soul into teaching school. Their classrooms are disciplined and orderly. Our children are well taught; best of all, they have another godly example to follow.

I have been blessed and encouraged by being invited to a tea party, a Sunday school Christmas party, or a meal for our family at single friends' houses.

All women are called by God to serve, help, and give to others.

"What meaningful ministries are you involved in? What do you do to bless others?"

· I try to do all I can to bring happiness to my home, my parents, my single sister, aged grandmother, and mentally handicapped aunt.

· I write weekly letters to the shut-ins, elderly, and the hurting and grieving; some were my former school teachers.

· I try to remember my fellow saints in prayer. I pray for those I sit beside in church.

· I bless my church by serving unselfishly in the classroom.

5. Queens of character learn to take all the difficulties and loneliness of life to God in prayer. They cast their burdens on the Lord, and find that He does sustain them (Ps. 55:22).

One of my dear friends says, "I have committed to the Lord who will take care of me when I am old. I trust He will take care of me."

The truth of the matter is that none of us know what the future holds or what tomorrow may bring. I could worry a lot about what would happen to my children and me if I were widowed. Yet, a single person does seem to be faced more starkly with the choice to trust God or to take matters into their own hands.

What are you going to do with your fears, worries, and loneliness? Trust that God is leading you. Leave tomorrow's problems for tomorrow.

Some singles go through a crisis from ages 35-45. They know their biological clock is running out. My friend Katie said, "Harder than giving up the dream of a husband is giving up the longing, the dream of my own little precious baby to care for and love." Some single women become so lonely they resort to having a baby out of wedlock so someone will need them. Yet, always, without exception, heartache is the result of immorality.

"We live in a confused world, a society that both fears commitment and suffers from alienation and loneliness."[6]

God's children do not need to view singleness as a curse. You are not destined to be alone. Not one of us is alone when we know the Lord! No, we are not alone. We have a community that surrounds us! We have the church and so many friends!

Loneliness can be viewed as an invitation to draw us to God. One lady testified, "I have lived alone for a number of years. I am learning to talk to God about anything and everything. Truly, God will never leave me or forsake me" (Heb. 13:5).

Rejoice in God's love and care. Isaiah 62:3-5 blessed me before I married, and I still find comfort in those verses…the Lord thy God delighteth in thee… as the bridegroom rejoices over the bride, so the Lord rejoices over you!!

To remain single can be considered a calling of God because one can be of greater service to God and the church. In contrast, a wife and mother's primary means of serving is the care and nurture of her husband and children.

"The unmarried woman careth for the things of the Lord, that she may be holy both in body and in spirit…" (I Cor. 7:34).

God is calling each of us to a closer and more intimate walk with Him!

"Whether single or married, we are all made with a desire to fellowship, to belong, to be accepted and loved. All of us need to find our identity in Jesus Christ alone, not in our husbands and friends. As we grow in our love and devotion to Christ, and in our thoughtfulness to others, we become more like the person God designed us to be."[7]

"What are some fears and difficulties singles face?"

· One of the hardest things about being single is loneliness, especially over holidays and Mother's Day.

· Living alone is no joke.

· Life is not as secure for a single woman, especially in thinking about the future.

· Married people think of the natural progression of life—children, grandchildren, always having a husband and children around you.

· Churches tend to be couple oriented. It is tough to not feel included. When most of my friends get married, they put me on the back shelf; we lose the closeness that we had before.

· What will happen to me? Who will take care of me when I am old and feeble? Will I have enough money? Planning ahead for retirement is a worry!

6. A queen of character is built up and strengthened by choosing edifying reading material.

We all need to stir up the flame of faith in our lives! Get in the Word. Read meaningful books and enjoy fellowship with others.

Avoid the wasteland of novels which tend to make you dissatisfied with your life.

Read, read, read! Here is a small list of recommended books: *Life is for Living* – Anita Yoder, *Through the Scent of Water* – Margaret Penner Toews, *Fine China is for Singles Too* – Lydia Brownback, *The Hiding Place, Tramp for the Lord* – Corrie ten Boom, *Quest for Love, Passion and Purity* – Elizabeth Elliot, *Awaiting the Dawn, Under His Wings, Whisper of Wings*, Dorcas Hoover.

Read biographies about missionaries. Be inspired by how others served the Lord and were faithful, triumphing over tremendous odds.

I don't feel stifled because I choose to read mostly nonfiction. My goal is reading material that will encourage, edify, and strengthen me in my walk with God.

. . . .

This chapter ends with the story of Barbie, a single lady who finds fulfillment and joy in the service of teaching, the work at an orphanage, and much more. She can be found ministering and serving, quietly for the Master, often behind the scenes.

YE SHALL KNOW THEM
–Dianna Overholt

There are different ways of knowing someone.

There is an I-know-you-intimately sort of thing that comes from family sharing of an afghan, a sofa, or a toaster. There is a shared-circumstance knowing from such things as rocking in the church nursery with babies the same age, or being survivors of an automobile accident. Some people you know through the creative expression of themselves such as a painting or a song. Sometimes people are known because they thrust themselves in the public eye. Others are discovered quite by accident.

Then there is the Biblical way of knowing someone. "By their *karpos*," said Jesus to His cluster of disciples on the mountainside, "ye shall know them." *Karpos* means fruit, of course, and more. Fruit that is plucked is the literal Greek meaning. This fruit, an extension of the tree, has fallen into the hands of the public. Look at the fruit cupped in your hands. Is it crisp and vibrant in color, or withered and knobby? Mother tree, we know your root system by the fruit we hold.

I almost missed knowing Barbie. I knew of her for some fifteen years—dark-haired, gentle, soft-spoken, a schoolteacher for ten years… She also had lived at two different foreign missions, working as a teacher and at an orphanage. Surface things, that's mostly what I knew. Because she is an in-the-background sort of person, I never really realized what a blessing she is.

That changed one Sunday evening, over the pulpit, no less. A brother wrapped up his topic by stating, "I'd like to close by reading a poem entitled 'I'm Free'."

I'm Free!

I'm free!
Free from the bonds that would shackle my soul,
Free from the fear-waves that over me roll,
Free from self-love (pride in disguise),
Free from being (in mine own eyes) wise,
Free from bitterness, that power of night,
Free from the "faith" dependent on sight.

I'm free!
Free as a bird flying high in the sky,
Free as the river that rushes by,
Free as a deer skipping over the hills,
Free as the songs that the mockingbird trills,
Free as the music of wind through the trees,
Free as the waves in the midst of the seas.

I'm free!
Free to laugh, to risk, and forgive,
Free to abandon myself—and live!
Free to be human—with His spirit inside,
Free to find Him the best place to hide.
Free to love, to hope, and to feel,
Free to believe in a God who is real.

I listened with tears slipping down my cheeks. I had been feeling so earth-bound and had been so full of longing. What beautiful expressions of freedom! Snatches of II Corinthians 3:17-18 came to mind. "Where the Spirit of the Lord is, there is liberty. But we all, with open face beholding… the glory of the Lord, are changed into the same image from glory to glory." *Whoever wrote that poem has undergone something significant*, I thought, *and emerged from it a little more transformed into glory!* It nudged me into doing what I had been putting off: to pour out my heart to God in acceptance of whatever He saw best for me.

By coincidence, I mentioned the impact the poem had on me to Barbie's sister. That's when I found out that Barbie had written the poem.

"I didn't know she wrote poetry!" I exclaimed.

"She hasn't shown her poetry to many besides family and close friends," her sister explained. (I wasn't surprised.) "You should read one that she wrote for our sister when she was going through a hard time."

I wanted to read it, and I'm sure you will too, so here it is:

The Best Defense
Could we but see with other eyes
The battle 'tween here and paradise
Behold God's angel hosts at war,
Not fainting, neither battle sore.

For each bright angel God did send,
His own dear children to defend,

When out from heaven's temple high,
He heard the voice and knew the cry.

Through faith alone we see and hear,
There's triumph in the heavenly sphere.
The very trouble that we face,
God changes to the good, by grace.

So we who need a sure defense,
When nothing here seems to make sense,
Will pray, believe, and let it rest;
God's on our side—and He fights best.

I started thinking about Barbie, and suddenly realized how apparent her godly fruit is. How many people have benefited from it?

Like the fruit of encouragement. One of the first times I remember meeting her was at a teachers' institute. As we chatted in the auditorium, she suddenly asked, "Could you excuse me for a minute? Brother Clarence is coming this way and I'd like to talk to him."

She held out her hand to the middle-aged minister, and after exchanging pleasantries, she remarked, "Brother Clarence, you probably don't remember me, but I responded at one of your revival meeting services in our church. I just want to thank you for allowing the Lord to use you."

A little shy myself, I was impressed with her "bravery" in approaching the minister. But more than that, it spoke to me of being an encourager.

She encourages me almost every time we meet. I don't see her often, perhaps once a year, but whenever we talk, she'll turn the conversation my way. "How is your writing?" she'll ask. If I don't watch it, she will skillfully keep the subject matter on me!

Her compassion is the next fruit I perceived. Some time after the teachers' institute, I went with her to an airport to meet a young woman who had just lost her husband four months earlier.

I stood there awkwardly, at loss for words, but Barbie hugged the widow and cried with her. Somehow she seems to be able to put herself in another's shoes.

Kindness is a fruit her students remember. "When I think back to being in her classroom, the first thing that comes to mind is her kindness," one student said. "The school board switched us to a different math curriculum and we were not up to the grade level it required. Math was rather difficult that year, but she didn't scold us or lose patience. She very kindly worked with us."

My sister also remembers the fruit of Barbie's kindness, or is it the fruit of love? (That's a sign of true fruit, when it comes in clusters and cannot be separated!) Having spent a summer at the Bethel Placement Center in Paltinis, Romania, she shared with me how quickly Barbie earned her respect. Barbie was at the orphanage from its very beginning to its end, a total of six years. My sister worked with four other Americans and three Romanians, caring for the twelve to fifteen children living there. "Barbie kept us all pulled together," my sister said. "She always treated us girls the same. We never saw her moody and she always seemed cheerful and had a good sense of humor. She kept things running smoothly behind the scenes in things like cleaning out drawers, reorganizing, or keeping the right size of clothes in the babies' closets."

There were two little sisters who lived at the orphanage for three years. When their mother had served her prison term and came to pick them up, it was Barbie who packed their dolls and special things for them to take home.

One baby girl was brought to the orphanage with spina bifida, an exposed spine that continually oozed. Doctors did not seem to know how to take care of it, and it looked so raw and sore that it was difficult to stomach. It was Barbie who literally formed a skin over the spine by constantly cleaning it and rubbing it with a special salve. She'd sing "Jesus Loves Me" as she worked on it, and little Ancuta came to love the song.

It has been a while since Barbie has lived for any length of time at home with her parents where her siblings and nieces and nephews are all close by. Her servant heart keeps her currently in Romania where she teaches school children and touches the needs of others by visiting lonely people, helping busy mothers, and praying for the church, all in the "background." "I am the vine," says Jesus. "He that abideth in me, and I in him, the same bringeth forth much fruit" (John 15:5).

By now you may be wondering if Barbie is perfect. I am sure she would be the first to tell you that she is not. We all have faults, but shouldn't our fruits overshadow them? The telling factor in one's life is not position, talents, or marital status. What reveals a person is his fruit, and fruit that has beautifully dropped into one's hands comes from a branch that is inseparably attached to the Vine.

I don't know Barbie in a daily, intimate way. I don't know if she likes to start the day with coffee or with conversation. We don't rock in the church nursery together. We don't even live in the same country. But yet I know her; I know her by her fruits, and those fruits have tasted sweet to many.

CHAPTER FIVE

And Martha
Served

L uke10:38-42, John 12:
I live with my brother Lazarus and my sister Mary in the town of Bethany. Jesus is one of our close friends. When He passes through our town, we always want Him to stop at our house for rest and refreshment. To just spend time together is such a joy!

Oh, we love it when Jesus comes, even though it usually includes His twelve disciples too. It's a lot of work, fixing food for all of those men, yet the presence of Jesus in our house is worth it all!

Nothing is too good for Jesus. Nothing! I try to do my best each time to be a perfect hostess for Him. He is always so appreciative, and never takes my efforts for granted.

One day when Jesus came, I wanted an extra special meal for Him and His disciples. Of late, we have been hearing that His life is in danger. It may now be perilous to entertain Him at our house, but I do not care, for I am willing to run any risk. Jesus will always be welcome here! The door of my house and the door of my heart will always be open to Jesus!

We were preparing a feast—Lazarus, Mary, and I—when Jesus came. He lovingly greeted us all by name. I continued with the work of preparing food. All the rest gathered around Jesus as He related various happenings of the times and the goodness and power of God.

I kept at my work, but began to feel smoldering resentment toward my sister. She sat quietly at Jesus' feet, leaving me to toil on alone. Finally I could stand it no longer. "Lord," I burst out, "don't you care that my sister is leaving all the work to me? Tell her to come and help me!"

I will never forget how Jesus looked at me and so tenderly spoke my name. "Martha, Martha," He said, "you are too anxious and worried about many things. Knowing me, hearing my words, sitting at my feet, that is what is most important and needful in life: Mary has discovered it. It shall not be taken away from her."

The words of Jesus smote my heart. Had I neglected what was most important? My much serving had not impressed the Master. Simple fare would have satisfied Him.

The light is dawning in my soul. Could it be that Jesus does not only want my service? Does He long for my heart's love and loyalty? Does He desire my undivided, undistracted time to sit at His feet?

"Oh Master, let me learn of Thee,
Oh, calm my heart and busy days.
Could my walk make others see,
That Jesus is the Lord of me?"

BEHOLD HOW HE LOVED HIM!

In the next account, Jesus had even greater impact on this unique home of three single siblings. Lazarus was ill. The sisters had sent for Jesus, saying, "Lord, the one whom you love is ill."

Jesus did not come until Lazarus had been buried: dead for four days. What a mind-troubling time that must have been. Why had not the Master come to them in their hour of greatest need?

Jesus told His disciples, "I am glad for your sakes that I was not there, to the intent that ye may believe; nevertheless let us go unto him" (John 11:15).

When Jesus finally came, He wept with the family. They were weeping as they took Jesus to the tomb of their brother.

There, God mightily revealed His power. Jesus said, "Take away the stone from the mouth of the cave." He prayed, and then cried with a loud voice, "Lazarus, come forth!" The dead man came out. What joy for that home! What a switch in emotions, from great sorrow to great joy! How they must have adored and worshiped Jesus. (Then too, many of the witnesses, such as Jewish leaders, friends, and relatives, finally believed on Him!)

In the next scene of this story, we find Jesus back at this home of His friends. A banquet was being prepared in His honor. Then we find these lovely words, "And Martha served" (John 12:2).

Martha serving again. What an honor to serve the Master!

Truly, all of God's women are called to serve. And how the Master loves and cares for us all!

"Oh how He loves you and me, oh how He loves you and me.
He gave His life, what more could He give?
Oh how He loves you, oh how He loves me,
Oh how He loves you and me.

CALM AND COLLECTED

What describes your life? Is it marked with worry and panic, fear and frenzy? Or is your life one of peace and calm? Is it a life of faith and trust in God?

God is a Rock, our shelter from the storms. He alone can give us peace and rest.

Come to God. Find calm, comfort, and rest.

Matthew 11:28: "Come unto me, all ye that labor and are heavy laden, and I will give you rest."

· Prayer doesn't remove every storm, but if we pray when the storms come, God will definitely calm us.

· We experience God's calm and peace when we abolish sin and ill attitudes.

· In everything that comes your way, accustom yourself to recognize the hand and will of God. Be calm.

A lady who found out she has incurable cancer stated, "It's all right. I am ready for whatever God has in store for me." What a lovely example of calm faith in God!!

I want to come to God more!

Give all your anxieties and cares to God.

I Peter 5:7: "Casting all your care upon him; for he careth for you."

What anxieties and cares that we struggle with should we give up to God? Cares of family, sick children, cares of aging parents, ill health, financial worries, questions about the future, what will my children face, worries about a possible death in the family, how would I cope? God does not call you to a life of fretfulness. You don't have to be a "worry woman." What do you have to lose by parting with your worries? Restless nights?

´In the past year, God has answered specific prayers about the care of my mother. It pays to pray! The prayer of faith gives us strength for the day and confidence for the future!

´Through all the trials of life, may our goal be to draw closer to God! He is our Rock of refuge and strength. We have no promise that God will give us smooth sailing all through life, but He does promise to be with us through it all!

Enemies of any color can never outwit God. God promises to take care of us. Psalm 31:15 states, "My times are in thy hands." A firm belief in God's faithfulness makes the difference between peace and panic!

I want to give God my cares and anxieties!

Look for the good in each day.

Philippians 4:8: "Finally, brethren, whatsoever things are true, whatsoever things are honest, whatsoever things are just, whatsoever things are pure, whatsoever things are lovely, whatsoever things are of good report; if there be any virtue, and if there be any praise, think on these things."

´Last summer on our trip to Texas, we parked at the airport

and took a shuttle to catch our flight. The shuttle bus driver was friendly. She asked, "Would you care for a drink?" She then gave each of us a cold water bottle. That blessed me.

One of our boys said, "I get so aggravated at my brother that I feel like doing something mean in return, but I won't because I am a Christian." Those words were a gem to my heart!

One morning, as I was reading my Bible in the sunroom, a brilliant hummingbird began flitting around the flowers outside my window. I felt God sent that tiny bird especially for me!

My small son throws his arms around me and gives me a kiss and a warm hug. "I love you, Mom," he whispers. What a gift!

I want to search for the good this year!

Make time for kindness.

Ephesians 4:32: "Be ye kind one to another." How can I be kind to my husband, my children, my friends, and anyone else who touches my life?

"Lord, give me inspiration and show me how."

Am I kind, especially at home? Margretta blessed me one day when she washed up the dishes without being told. That same day, Micah had washed the breakfast dishes cheerfully. Markus said I was kind because I played a game with him.

One morning, Mark heated the water for my tea. It's a kindness when I serve him fragrant coffee early in the morning. I appreciate all the back rubs he gives me!

The little things really count! After all, you can sit on a mountain, but not on a tack! Try kindness in many little ways. You will be amazed how kindness does come back! I want to make time for kindness in all my days!

May you enjoy peace and rest as you come to God. Give Him your anxieties and cares. Search for the good in each day, and make time for kindness.

Stages of Life

When each day is filled to the brim with caring for small ener-
getic children, it is hard to imagine that the day will come when
I will choose what I want to do, and what I should do each day.
There is coming a day when my house will be quiet.

After my dad passed away, I made it a goal to frequently call
my mother. One morning when I called her, I said, "Mom, what
are you going to do today?"

"I want to finish reading a book about Paraguay, and Aunt
Lydia invited me to come over this afternoon to help her with
some comfort kits she is making to send to Romania," my mom
told me.

What a quiet, peaceful morning for my mom, and yet living
alone can be difficult. To be loved and needed is indeed one of
life's greatest joys!

Contrast that to my morning. Monday is the busiest morning
with mountains of laundry to attend to, six school lunches to
pack, breakfast to prepare, and always the endeavor to send the
five children happily off to school. I kiss Mark good-bye as he
heads out for another day of teaching high school.

The laundry needs to be finished. Wash the dishes. Sweep
the floor forevermore! I like things to be reasonably neat. It pays
to take time to put the house in order each morning. I also do
countless other small things, mend, bake, and plan meals.

My five-year-old helps hang out the laundry. We take time to
read stories and take a walk. In the afternoon when he naps, a
sixty-minute space of quietness is a blessed treat indeed.

A mother needs to give and give and give. I greatly need to
be quiet at Jesus' feet each day so I can be filled and have a joyful
spirit to continue giving and giving to my family.

When people ask me what I do, I am happy to say I am not
employed away from home, though I do like to assure them that
I WORK! My work at home is high on my priority list. Meeting
my family's needs is paramount! I once read that what I do inside
the walls of my home is the most important work I will ever do!

One of my friends, whose children are grown and gone, says, "I try to be alert for ways I can minister to others. On days when I do not have a lot that has to be done, I like to sew crafts. I also like to be available to help my married daughters when I can."

My busiest time of life was when I had four preschoolers. Now we have four teenagers, and two who are younger in our house. Life is one continual challenge!

What a stage of life this is for my mother. She struggles with ill health. She wonders why she is still here, and what she can do for the Lord.

Somehow, we must learn to embrace each day as a gift from God, and throw our whole heart and soul into doing our best. Then life will not just pass us by; we will have lived well, enjoyed each stage, and brightened the corner where God has placed us!

We have this moment to hold in our hands,
And to touch as it slips through our fingers like sand,
Yesterday's gone, and tomorrow may never come,
But we have this moment today!

Time for Friends?

I thought my spring days were nearly too full and busy to plan a housewarming for my friend Mary, who had recently moved. But I kept thinking about it. One Sunday morning, when I was meditating and praying, I thought about it again.

When God keeps bringing something to my mind over and over, then I try to stop, listen, and do it.

I called Mary and asked her when our Sunday school class could come for a visit. Monday, the very next day, was fine! Mary said she would make tea and coffee; I told her we would bring finger foods.

I called our Sunday school teacher and asked her to announce a get-together at Mary's apartment for Monday afternoon at two. I also asked the teacher to tell each one to bring a thought to share about friendship, and a few jars of their home-canned food for Mary.

Monday was a breezy, warm day. Lots of work in the garden, greenhouse, and flower beds beckoned me. I had a huge laundry, too. Yet I went to Mary's house. It was interesting to see where she lived.

Ten ladies sat around Mary's kitchen table. We drank hot tea and gourmet coffee from her pretty collection of exquisite teacups. It was special to fellowship and eat good food together. I thought about—and told them—that twenty-two years ago I likely didn't know any of them, and today I thank God they are my friends.

It was refreshing and encouraging to hear each one's thoughts about friendship. We sang the song, "There's Not a Friend Like the Lowly Jesus."

I went back home to my work, thankful for the nice time I had with my friends!

May you always find three welcomes in life,
In a garden during the summer,
At a fireside during the winter,
And whatever the season,
In the kind eyes of a friend.
(from the booklet, *The Joys of Friendship*)

. . . .

Martha served. In this story we see that Ada served. We all have different talents and abilities. Yet, in some way, all of us are called to serve.

ONLY ONE ADA
—Faith Sommers

"Lover of hospitality" is the first thing I think of when I remember all the times I have spent with Victor and Ada Schlabach. If we needed a place to stay, to eat, to play, to visit, that was the home. We grew up with their family. I can't imagine life without them.

When I was only three years old, my sister and I stayed with the Schlabachs while our parents went to the annual ministers' meeting. I enjoyed it so much that I told my mother, "When Victors are tired of my sister, she can move back home; I'll just stay!"

Ada loved to help out with other people's children. My mother had her hands full with a row of lively children, besides being a minister's wife. While my dad was preaching, Ada often cared for one of Mom's little ones.

My earliest memories are of Ada and her jolly laugh. She made any activity fun. Even normally boring, distasteful jobs like butchering chickens or shelling bushels of peas. She would start telling stories, and soon our hands would fly with our work while our minds traveled with her tales. Laughter was an inevitable result, and we discovered, to our amazement, that the job at hand was nearly finished. She had the gift of making the best out of any circumstance.

She rarely had blue days, or else we didn't notice! If I was feeling sad, she would cheer me by her positive words. Even now, as an adult, when I need encouragement—or perhaps a chuckle—a call to Ada will do the trick. Her favorite verse is, "Rejoice in hope" (Romans 5:2). That certainly is her motto.

She is one of the "giving-est" people I know. One delight my five sisters and I enjoyed was receiving a bag of dresses Ada's girls had outgrown. The fabric was much more up-to-date than ours, or so we thought, and the colors were lovely. She knew my mother was hard-pressed to keep us in dresses, and though she didn't really care to sew, this was a wonderful way to help our family.

Recently, she told me about a little lunch stand she does with her grandchildren. Years ago, she set up a small food stand for the oldest girls in her son's family. She promised the younger girls she would do the same with them sometime. They called her one day last summer, and asked if they could have their lunch stand. "Sure," was the expected response. She baked cookies and fixed barbecue beef and ham and cheese sandwiches. She called a neighbor and told her what the little girls were planning. The neighbor sent her work crew over, and oh, what fun it was! The girls set a table in the yard, and bounced into the house for hot sandwiches whenever a customer stopped. This was so "typical Ada," and it warmed my heart. Now, although we live a disheartening 1900 miles apart, this reassured me that Ada has not changed!

I remember cold, snowy days when we gathered at her house for hot chocolate, and of course lots of delicious food. Once, a blizzard was the cause for the cancellation of school, but it didn't keep our family at home! We piled into my dad's big four-wheel drive pickup truck and carefully crept along the snow-drifted roads to the Schlabach house. I clearly remember the happy shouts of welcome we received as we arrived.

"Here, throw your coats on the hall table. We'll set your boots in the garage so they won't be too cold when you leave. Now just come on in and get warm. First, let's have something to eat!" Ada welcomed us all.

There weren't only a few of us! Oh, what a merry time we had.

I'm sure we wrecked the house in our lively games, but Ada had much patience. In fact, she often suggested games and played dominoes or Memory with us. She was a courageous teacher for little ones who were just learning their numbers. She would patiently explain the rules again and again.

Even though their children numbered four, she would have been a mother suited for a dozen! She loves children, and children love her. She has a wonderful gift of making little people happy. She cuddles children of all sizes, and though she never gave birth to any of her own, her love is encompassing and glorious.

One time, she shared a few struggles that they faced in the adoption process. Oh, the rude remarks some folks made! Ada admitted she shed many tears those long-ago days, but there was no trace of bitterness in her voice as she told us about it. Watching their family convinced me that an adoptive mother and father love their children just as much as birth parents do. Their oldest daughter says there are times she forgets Ada is not her birth mother. What a beautiful picture of our lives as Christians. We are adopted into the family of God. We are secure in His love and we belong completely to our Father God!

In the early 1980s, the church which the Schlabachs were a part of decided to colonize, or start a new church outreach. This was no minor decision, as one thousand miles separated Pennsylvania and Missouri. Not only were they leaving all their extended family behind, but it must have been especially hard to leave their mothers (both Victor and Ada's fathers had passed away previously). But I don't remember any complaining; much more, Ada's typical response of thanksgiving and joy permeated those early days of eking out a living in a land that was often dry and very stony.

Hard, barren years describes the first years in Missouri. Farming and gardening took on a completely different perspective from the Eastern ways. The ladies tried new kinds of seeds that would withstand the harsh warm winds and fierce sunshine of the Midwest. The men planted crops and harvested hay after clearing acres of rocks and occasionally trees. They found the humidity a challenge. The hay would not always dry fast enough to be baled before a sudden summer thunderstorm struck.

They didn't give up! The men worked construction jobs to pay the bills, and taught the children the glories and grimies of growing up on a dairy farm. Our church was small. Sometimes everybody worked in the hayfield gathering up bales, and we always put up sweet corn together. Once, each family sold a calf to raise enough money to pay the school teacher! There was a warm feeling of togetherness and love that is hard to duplicate in a large congregation.

With the passing of years, our church grew so much that we colonized again. Then seven years later, yet again. Although Victor and Ada weren't called to move away, they were encouragers and firm supporters to those who moved. They baby-sat, fixed meals, delivered loads, and showed they cared in creative ways. It was a very sad day for my family when we realized we would no longer be in the same church as Victor and Ada were! "There is just one Victor Ada."

Though the Schlabach family wasn't wealthy, they always gave tithes to the Lord. I recall Victor once saying that if you don't give to the Lord when you are poor and think you can ill afford it, then you probably won't give when you can afford it! "God always provides," was his testimony. He took Ephesians 4:28 literally: "Work with your own hands that ye may have to give to him that needeth."

The deep love for the Lord is evident in Ada's life. She is a great example for the younger women to look to. We learn so much from observing and asking questions from those older than us. Although life hasn't always been easy, Ada's faith and joy in God will always inspire me.

CHAPTER SIX

A Life Transformed

M ary Magdalene. Wretched. Forlorn. Miserable. Someone the world deemed unimportant.

Her life was full of depression and defeat. That she appeared discouraged and disheveled was no surprise, for she was possessed by seven devils (Luke 8:2). She was bound by Satan. What an awful plight. But Mary was RADICALLY CHANGED BY JESUS.

The Scriptures do not record what Mary Magdalene's symptoms of demon possession were. Ancient records reveal that some demon-possessed people were exceeding fierce and uncontrollable persons, striking fear in the hearts of others. Mental disorders or disruptive, painful illnesses were often blamed on a demon.

Then Jesus came!

He came to:

· destroy the works of the devil
· preach the Gospel to the poor
· heal the brokenhearted
· preach deliverance to the captives
· recover the sight of the blind
· set at liberty them that are bruised (to release the oppressed)
· comfort all that mourn
· give His life a ransom for many

When Jesus was here on the earth, He and His followers cast out many, many devils. The ministry of Jesus has power over the forces of sin and Satan. The ministry of Jesus gives fresh hope and help to the fainting hearts of those who seek Him.

How did Mary Magdalene come to meet Jesus that wonderful day when He cast those seven awful demons out of her? Did they meet by chance, or was it by divine appointment? We don't know the details, but we do know she was miraculously changed. She went on to become a woman with a purpose, a devoted disciple who willingly followed Jesus and ministered to Him. Her name is mentioned twelve times in the Scriptures.

Mary witnessed Jesus' miracles.

She heard His sermons.

She profited from His teachings.

Her heart overflowed with gratitude that Jesus did not confine His ministry to the public world of male dominance.

Every writer of the Gospels mentions Mary Magdalene in the record of those who were present that awful day when Jesus Christ was crucified. Many followers fled in that fearful, never-to-be-forgotten event, but several faithful women, including Mary Magdalene, courageously stayed at the cross, not ashamed to openly identify with their Lord!

John pictures her as standing with Mary, the mother of Jesus. We can imagine her upholding and comforting His mother, sharing her sorrow and agony of heart.

Hours later, the women were still watching when Joseph of Arimathea took the body of Jesus down from the cross. They followed the procession. They viewed the sepulchre, where the body of their beloved Master was put to rest.

The women prepared spices and ointments for His body. Then they rested on that saddest of Sabbath days.

After the Sabbath, Mary Magdalene's courage and dedication is evidenced by her coming in the predawn darkness, with other women, to the tomb of Jesus. Imagine their shock and dismay at finding the tomb empty.

God had not forsaken these faithful women. They were the first to receive the wondrous message from two shining angels that Jesus is risen. "Remember how Jesus spake to you," said the angels, "that He would be crucified, and the third day rise again?"

They remembered His words!

The sun arose over a wakening world, dispelling the gloom of night and their grief. Mary Magdalene and the others rushed to tell the eleven disciples the wondrous news that has echoed down through the centuries, "JESUS CHRIST IS RISEN!"

But where was Jesus? Mary Magdalene returns to the sepulchre, her deep love for Jesus evidenced by her weeping. Looking into the tomb again, she beholds two angels in white, sitting where the body of Jesus had lain. They wonder why she is weeping. She replies, "They have taken away my Lord, and I know not where they have laid Him."

While Mary was still weeping, she encountered Jesus, but did not recognize Him till He spoke her name, "Mary."

Her sorrow and despair turned to joy. Her hope was not in a mere man, but in the infallible, risen, living Savior of all mankind, Jesus Christ the Son of God!

"Master!" she cried.

I imagine Mary falling at the feet of Jesus, overcome with the reality of the resurrection, the reality of wonderful life after the cruelty of the awful crucifixion. "Master, my Master," Mary sobbed.

Jesus told her not to touch Him. "I have not yet ascended to the Father," He said.

Mary Magdalene, out of whom He had cast seven devils, was honored and rewarded by being the first to see the risen Lord. Then Jesus gave her a mission which she faithfully fulfilled, "Go tell my brethren that I ascend unto my Father, and your Father; and to my God, and your God."

Mary went and told the disciples that she had seen the Lord, and that He had spoken these things to her.

Mary Magdalene then disappears from the scriptural record.

She is not mentioned in Acts as being with the believers, as the mother of Jesus was. But very likely she was there. Her ardent faith and staunch support of the ministry of Jesus may well have helped to fan the flame of life and belief in her risen Lord and Savior, Jesus Christ.

Was Mary married? Scripture gives no clue that she was. Whether married or single, Jesus was her all in all.

Mary loved her Lord with a passion. After she met Jesus, we find nothing of her turning back, or wavering in her commitment to Him. Could that be said of you and me?

VICTORY IN JESUS!

I Peter 2:25: "For ye were as sheep going astray; but are now returned to the Shepherd and Bishop of your souls."

Each one of us was a lost sheep before we found the Lord. True repentance is turning away from sin. It is going home to the arms of our loving heavenly Father. Repentance is choosing to obey the Lord. Your love and allegiance is given to God instead of to self and the world. To those who seek Him and follow His ways God gives power, peace, and victory.

Every person who ever lived has hurts and struggles. You may have . . .

· come from a home where a parent or a family member is mentally ill. Your family has suffered deeply and few know about it and fewer yet understand.

· come from a broken home and your heart is bruised and battered. (Don't believe the devil's whispers that your life has to be a similar one of defeat and disobedience to the Lord.)

· suffered sexual abuse and feel your future holds continual struggles, sickness, and defeat.

· fallen into immorality.

· been tempted to think, "There is no hope for me. No one knows my secret sins. It is too difficult to confess."

Remember, God knows it all. There is nothing you can hide

from Him. Do not believe the lie from the devil that no one needs to know. The enemy of our souls wants you to waste years and months hiding. Don't listen to his lies.

"Know ye not that the unrighteous shall not inherit the kingdom of God? Be not deceived; neither fornicators, nor idolaters, nor adulterers, nor effeminate, nor abusers of themselves with mankind, nor thieves, nor covetous, nor drunkards, nor revilers, nor extortioners, shall inherit the kingdom of God. And such were some of you; but ye are washed, but ye are sanctified, but ye are justified in the name of the Lord Jesus, and by the Spirit of our God" (I Corinthians 6:9-11).

Jesus is waiting with open arms of love. Become free and forgiven by washing in His blood. Confess your sin to God. Find a trusted godly friend. Share, confess, and become whole in the amazing love and mercy of God.

"Confess your faults one to another, and pray one for another, that ye may be healed. The effectual fervent prayer of a righteous man availeth much" (James 5:16).

The hardest thing to do may be to forgive those who hurt us. We must forgive. To experience God's love and forgiveness we must forgive.

In her book *Committed to the Covenant* Liz Lapp shared how she had a desperate desire for her children to walk in purity. She encourages parents:

"Do everything in your power to promote purity in your home and in the lives of your children.

"Do all you can to prevent your children and teenagers from becoming involved in pornography, fornication, uncleanness, lasciviousness, defrauding, and sexual abuse, or bestiality. Many children are robbed of their innocence or purity by these sins, resulting in lifelong scars. Too many repeat the sins of their ancestors.

"I did not believe the sins of one generation had to follow another, but how was the cycle broken?"

Liz Lapp's husband left her with three children. He left a God-fearing woman for an ungodly one. She was deeply concerned that her son would not follow in his father's footsteps of sin. She took him with her to visit a caring, godly pastor.

"He counseled my son to acknowledge the sins of his father, as the children of Israel did in Nehemiah 9:2 and Leviticus 26:40, so they would not be visited upon him. My son was not asking forgiveness for his father's sins, he was taking a personal stand against repeating them in his own life. The pastor earnestly prayed with my son, asking God to help him walk according to the Word and live in the power of the Holy Spirit. Along with this I bathed my children in prayer and did all I could to exemplify a life of purity. I believed these weapons, in this warfare, to be mighty through God to the defeating of the enemy of our souls according to II Corinthians 10:4. This gave me hope for the oncoming generation, and today I see God showing His mercy toward them that love Him."[8]

....

This story about Andy and Antonia is precious to me because they are dear friends and family in the Lord. Their story portrays the goodness and mercy of God to all who need a Savior.

COMING HOME

My friend Antonia showed me a picture from years ago. She was sitting at a table, her black wavy hair cascading over her shoulders. In front of her was a bottle of beer. I was amazed. Today Antonia is so different. Today she walks with God.

Antonia's parents grew up in Greece. Starvation stalked them through difficult times. Life was much easier when they moved to the United States. Her parents were hardworking, respectable people, though not living for the Lord. Their children were loved and secure. They did not have a car, but one uncle always picked them up for church. Seeds were being planted for the Lord in the heart of one little girl. When she was in second grade her sister helped her pray. She asked the Lord to come into her heart.

In her youth, Antonia dated a number of different men. She

was in a serious relationship for over three years. Eventually that man became jealous and very possessive. When she told him she wanted to break up, he was upset. One day he became violent and grabbed her by her throat. Antonia was terrified.

Today she is so grateful and realizes it was by the mercy of God that that relationship came to an end.

Outgoing, friendly, talkative, and bubbly describes Antonia. Andy was one of her brother's friends. Antonia was always congenial and talked to his friends. The friendship with Andy gradually developed into something deeper than just her brother's friend.

Andy moved out to Colorado and was at an Olympic Training Center. He loved the feel of lifting those heavy weights. He was strong and all the weight lifting hardened his muscles even more. Andy and Antonia would call each other. They could talk for hours on the phone. Antonia felt that she had found her soul mate and a very physically appealing man.

He was polite, just so comfortable and nice. Andy was delighted that such a pretty girl would go out with him. They dated for years. One day they went to look at a house that was for sale out in the country and decided to do a joint purchase.

Earlier Antonia's two older sisters had moved in with their boyfriends. Her parents were unhappy about that. Eventually though they became accustomed to it. They decided that is what everyone in this country does. They did not mind it much when Antonia and Andy decided to just move in together, plus they just really liked Andy.

Andy's parents were not thrilled about the arrangement, though it was a common practice (for the unsaved as they were). Andy says he had a rebellious attitude and was not very concerned with his parents' view on the matter.

In her heart though, Antonia felt troubled and guilty about just living together. She believed in God and knew living this way was against His will and Word.

Through the witness of a woman who prayed with her, Antonia

recommitted her life to God. She felt that she was a child of God. The Holy Spirit was nudging her heart, though she was not yet living in obedience.

Andy says, "I was from a typical American Protestant, once-saved always-saved church. I thought I was saved because I had once prayed a prayer asking the Lord to come into my life. I thought I was saved, and yet I was still drinking, cursing, and smoking. I'm ashamed of that now. I was living with my girl-friend and in no hurry to get married. We were very much in the world. We had worldly desires, worldly gods, and things were getting worse and worse."

During this time Antonia was finishing up her schooling to become an occupational therapist. They were busy. At times they'd discuss marriage.

Eventually Andy felt it was the time to get married. Antonia was delighted when Andy finally asked her to marry him. She was overjoyed to promise to be his wife. Andy gave her a ring, which is normal in their culture. They felt a ring solidified their commitment.

GOD KNOWS WHERE YOU ARE

Andy, a strong, stocky man, thought he had his life under control—very much in control. He thought he could handle anything. Yet, it bothered him that he could not stop smoking. He tried numerous times, but he was addicted. He just craved those cigarettes. Antonia did not like that. She only smoked occasionally. Frequenting bars was a pleasure to her husband too. He got silly when he drank enough, but he never did get violent. For that she was very grateful. After a stressful day at work, Antonia was not happy to see him come home with a six-pack. She knew it was the way her husband liked to relax.

In each of our lives are two distinct powers. God and Satan. Who will we follow? Whose voice will we obey?

Antonia knew that if they ever had children she wanted them

to be a family that goes to church. She longed to be a Christian family. She wanted her children to know the Lord. (It is amazing how often God grants us our true heart's desire, when that desire is one that pleases the Lord!) Some days though she felt scared, especially when she saw Andy studying literature about Buddhism and other religions.

One day, much to her delight, Andy said, "Let's go to church on Sunday." By then they were married and had a sweet baby girl.

Antonia felt like saying, "Where did that come from? Why do you want to go to church?" But she was afraid she would spoil something good and so she kept quiet. She really did want to attend church. She had been praying and wishing that Andy, her strong Andy, would come to the Lord.

Together they looked in their phone book. They decided to attend a nearby Baptist church on Sunday.

WHERE ART THOU?

"Where art thou" (Genesis 3:9)? God asked Adam that question when he sinned. God was asking Andy, "Where art thou?" That is a powerful question. "Where art thou?" God knows where you are! God was calling Andy and Antonia.

He is calling each of us to turn from our wicked ways and seek His face. Are we willing to listen? Are we willing to let go of the things God will show us when we earnestly seek Him?

Andy felt the call of God on his life. "Oh, Lord, come into my heart," he sincerely prayed one day. Andy testifies, "I believe that He did." He felt God was telling him, "Andy, I can use you. First I have to break you."

"God has worked wonders in our lives. We want to honor Him," is their testimony today.

Isaiah 51:1 is a verse that means a lot to Andy. "Hearken to me, ye that follow after righteousness, ye that seek the Lord; look to the rock whence ye are hewn, and to the hole of the pit whence ye are digged."

Conviction came to the heart of Andy that his habit of smoking was not pleasing to the Lord. He was addicted to tobacco. He knew he could not quit on his own strength. He pleaded with God. "Please take this away from me." God heard his sincere cry. God took the craving for cigarettes away from Andy. It is amazing, awesome, and incredibly astounding what God can do!

One day Andy was showing one of his friends from church through their house. When his friend saw the bar Andy had built, a deep feeling of shame came over Andy. God was working. Andy felt a need to apply Scripture to his life. Sin was becoming exceeding sinful (Romans 7:13).

The next day, led by God, Andy ripped that bar out of his house. He took it to the back yard and grabbed his ax. His muscular arms smashed the bar to smithereens. He struck a match to the wood. The fire destroyed the remains of his bar. The smoke ascended to the heavens. He had sacrificed his pet sin as an offering to God.

Andy was not done yet. He came back into the house and grabbed up an armful of booze off their shelves. He took it to the back yard and dumped it out. The brown liquid foamed and soaked away into the soil. He came in for another load and did not quit till a thousand dollars' worth of booze had oozed away. He made such a clean sweep that he grabbed up Antonia's bottle of cooking wine and dumped that too.

Andy resolved that by the grace, help, and power of God he would stand firm and never touch strong drink again. He asked the Lord to take his desire for alcohol away. GOD DID IT!

All that liquor killed the green grass. For a long time there was a round brown spot on their lawn near the back porch. It was a reminder that sin kills and destroys. It was a reminder of his resolve to live for God.

Martin Luther said, "To do so no more is the truest repentance."

Andy and Antonia became dissatisfied with the church they had been attending for a year. They found another church which they hoped would be more scriptural.

Antonia stood amazed at all the changes in the man she dearly loved. God was working in her heart too. She searched the Scriptures, and more and more she was becoming uncomfortable with her jewelry. She cross-examined the Scriptures. She asked herself, "Am I willing to stand out for God?"

I Timothy 2:9: "In like manner also, that women adorn themselves in modest apparel, with shamefacedness and sobriety; not with braided hair, or gold, or pearls, or costly array."

I Peter 3:3: "Whose adorning let it not be that outward adorning of plaiting the hair, and of wearing of gold, or of putting on of apparel."

The Word of God was speaking to her. *Do not be known by your adornment, but by your modesty and obedience to my commands.*

Antonia asked herself some searching questions about choices she was making.

1. What is my motive for changing?
2. Where did it come from?
3. Is it glorifying God?

Would she obey or disobey truths from the Word of God that were becoming clear to her?

All of us need to remember that for every child of God, obedience is the pathway to growth and victory with God.

One day she felt like she was wrestling with God like Jacob when he wrestled all night with the angel. Her ears were pierced, four holes in one ear, two in the other. Taking off her large gaudy earrings was not so difficult. She looked in the mirror. "But these tiny diamond earrings are ones my husband gave me," she reasoned. She went back to her work, then back to the mirror. "These are just small pretty diamonds," she vacillated. "I should take them off…yet these are just dainty and cute…"

Finally she just willed her hands to take them off. She felt a peace and blessing from the Lord.

God leads His dear children along. He leads gently. God shows us a little at a time things that are not good. We need to grow and change. No matter how long we have followed Christ there are still areas that God works on to purify us and draw us nearer to Him. We dare not come to the point that we sigh with a proud satisfaction and think, now I have arrived. We need God each day. We need to continue to grow.

II Corinthians 3:18: "But we all, with open face beholding as in a glass the glory of the Lord, are changed into the same image from glory to glory, even as by the Spirit of the Lord."

One summer while vacationing, God led them right to the home of people who loved the Lord. They were invited to tent meetings and were deeply touched by Donnie Brenneman's sincere preaching. They were shown hospitality and invited to people's homes for a meal and for fellowship. They went home amazed, blessed, and strengthened.

Antonia kept thinking about how she dressed. She wanted to follow the Word and be modest. She also wanted Andy to be comfortable with her clothes. He was not ready for major changes just yet.

A good marriage is like our relationship with God. We must give it time. We must be patient, determined, and not give up. Women need to learn to let their husbands lead the home. Learn to wait, pray, and be patient before the Lord.

Antonia often wore her hair up. She was not a high maintenance lady, but very practical. She believed the Scripture that said her hair was for her husband (I Corinthians 11). She sought God. She prayed, "Lord, make Your Word clear to me." For a long time she searched the Scriptures. She read. She studied for months. She wanted to be obedient to God's Word.

She felt lonely, yet convinced when she decided to wear a veiling. Andy gave his consent. It was not an easy step. They were scared, yet courageous and willing to follow the Lord.

Today Andy is praising God that his wife submitted to following the Scripture on wearing a veiling. He believes she will be blessed.

Matthew 7:21: "Not everyone that saith unto me, Lord, Lord, shall enter into the kingdom of heaven; but he that doeth the will of my Father which is in heaven."

Hospitality, cooking, and entertaining guests at their house are things Antonia loves. She is warm and welcoming. Her home is cozy and comfortable. Andy is friendly and congenial too. One day they invited some family members for a Sunday dinner. A sister-in-law was known for dressing indiscreetly. She would brazenly wear low-cut tops. It was that way whenever she came to their house.

Andy observed the immodesty in his home that day. He did not want that for his family. When their guests left he told his wife he is okay with her wearing a modest dress. Antonia chose to wear dresses with wide skirts and a modest bodice.

I John 2:3: "Hereby we do know that we know him, if we keep his commandments."

A verse that means a lot to Antonia is Romans 1:16: "For I am not ashamed of the gospel of Christ, for it is the power of God unto salvation to everyone that believeth, to the Jew first, and also to the Greek." She confided that when God shows her things in her life that she should change she wants to and often feels compelled to obey. The hardest part is the thought, "What will people think?"

You become what you are looking at. I need to keep asking myself, "Am I looking at the world or at the Word of God?"

One of Antonia's favorite songs is:

Turn Your Eyes Upon Jesus
Turn your eyes upon Jesus,
Gaze full in His wonderful face.
And the things of earth
Will grow strangely dim
In the light of His glory and grace.

Hebrews 12:2-3: "Looking unto Jesus the author and finisher of our faith; who for the joy that was set before him endured the cross, despising the shame, and is set down at the right hand of the throne of God. For consider him that endured such contradiction of sinners against himself, lest ye be wearied and faint in your minds."

God gave Andy and Antonia three lovely, lively children. They would have loved to have another child. Antonia was delighted to find out that she was pregnant again. Then she had a miscarriage. It was a difficult time. She felt very emotional and vulnerable. She knew she needed to give all her sorrow over to the Lord. Of course she needed time to recover, rest, and relax.

Here is what she told me, "Saturday I stayed in bed all morning. I was not sure if I had given over all my sorrow to God yet. I prayed. I finally told Satan that he will not steal my joy. I hopped out of bed, and praise God, I have felt good ever since."

More changes were on their horizons. They found a church an hour from their home. A church where the people endeavored to live out the principles in the Word of God. A church that believed in hospitality. At the other churches they had attended they would invite couples to their house for lunch, but seldom did anyone ever invite them over. In five years' time they had only one invitation. Now the fellowship they found was sweet.

It was a weighty decision to give up their wedding bands. Antonia finally came to the place that she wanted to take hers off. Andy says, "I never was a big jewelry guy. It seemed like every nice piece of jewelry I got would be lost or stolen. I have to say around the time Antonia wanted to take hers off, my wedding band became very irritating. I started to have a rash around my finger, though I had worn it for years. I thought maybe this was a sign, so I stopped wearing it."

God pricked both of their consciences about television. Andy felt like he couldn't watch this show, don't watch that show. Finally he said, "This is it!" Andy states that the violence, nudity, and homosexuality on TV is an attempt to desensitize people to sin. It is an attempt to make sin normal.

Isaiah 5:20: "Woe unto them that call evil good, and good evil; that put darkness for light, and light for darkness; that put bitter for sweet, and sweet for bitter."

When they got rid of the TV, the children whined, yet they soon adapted. That change in their home was a blessing. Their children would more often play together nicely, and sit contentedly reading a book. It made a significant difference in their lives. Before, their children couldn't sit still for ten minutes at a time.

Andy shares, "My extended family today is completely separated from the church to the point of unbelief and a constant never-ending unrest. Homosexuality is in my family. I never imagined it would get that bad."

Isaiah 57:20-21: "But the wicked are like a troubled sea, when it cannot rest, whose waters cast up mire and dirt. There is no peace, saith my God, to the wicked."

Antonia shared, "Our families do not honor God. They are lost. There are drugs and abuse. Sin is rampant. Andy's parents did not talk to the one grandmother for thirteen years. My brothers do not go to church. At least our parents are not divorced."

Oh, there are such rich blessings when we follow the Lord and walk in His ways.

I like how Andy expressed himself about his wife. "I always loved Antonia. I couldn't have imagined the Lord would bring us so much closer than we were before we were saved. There are times I miss her dearly when I have a long day or a tough day. I am so relieved to see her sweet face when I come home. I am truly blessed."

Today Antonia still admires her husband's strength. What she admires most though is his walk and strength with God. (True strength is to know and obey God.) She thanks the Lord as she observes all the changes and the victory both of them are experiencing.

I John 2:14: "I have written unto you, young men, because ye are strong, and the Word of God abideth in you, and ye have overcome the wicked one."

Matthew 10:37: "He that loveth father or mother more than

me is not worthy of me; and he that loveth son or daughter more than me is not worthy of me."

Antonia told me, "God is growing us. He is taking us farther from family and all the people we loved. That is not easy. We feel a deep sadness for those who are lost in sin. Pray for us that we would be a true witness to our family and our friends who need the Savior. God is with us. He does not leave us alone. He has given us many new friends in the Lord. We are still living here, but our heart and affections are with the Lord."

"Most people think we have fallen off our rockers," Andy confided. "I have never had so much peace about what I am doing. What's best is I can tell that the Lord is working on me every day. I have seen rewards. Prayers have been answered. Lives have been changed. I have had open challenges by family and mocking by co-workers. We have made changes as the Lord has convicted us. God has opened my eyes. I want to keep on growing. I can not change what I have done in the past, but by the help of God I can change what I am doing now."

Andy and Antonia's story is not finished yet. Your story, my story, is not finished either. God keeps working to transform us, drawing us nearer to His heart, till He calls us home.

May each of us continue to seek God and grow as we look to Jesus.

CHAPTER SEVEN

Cured, Confirmed, and Comforted

The account of this destitute woman who in desperation reached out to Jesus and found not only the physical healing she longed for, but also spiritual healing, should be an encouragement to all of us to seek the Lord. Long for Him. Reach out to Him, and find Him sufficient to meet all our needs.

Imagine being ill for twelve years and spending all that you had. Imagine becoming impoverished in your search for health and, like an illusive dream, your health did not improve; rather, it became definitely worse! Imagine suffering many things at the hands of many physicians (Matthew 9:20-22, Mark 5:24-34, Luke 8:43-48).

Imagine having a disease that would render you ceremonially unclean. An issue of blood that would shut you out of the courts of the Lord's house; shut you out for twelve years!

Imagine this uncleanness, which was viewed so seriously that if anyone touched you, your bed, or your couch they too were unclean.

In short, imagine being ill, untouched, unloved, unnoticed, and unwanted.

This poor, thin, destitute woman likely thought she would never be strong and healthy again. Although she could have given up, her small flicker of hope was fanned into a large flame of faith when she began to hear accounts of Jesus. She heard how great multitudes yearned to touch Jesus. Wherever Jesus was, great multitudes in the city, the villages, or the country sought to touch Him, or at least the hem of His robe. Virtue went out of Him and healed all who touched Him. She heard of multitudes thronging Jesus and becoming whole!

Because she lived in a time when women were looked down on, she felt she could not speak openly to Christ about her disease. Yet, she believed in His healing power. She believed that only a timid touch would heal and cure her. Only a touch! It became her consuming passion to find the Lord Jesus.

One eventful day, a pressing crowd surrounded Jesus. Jairus had pled with Him to come to his house and lay His hands on his beloved daughter, who was deathly ill. Jesus was on His way. A great throng of people followed Him.

Lost in that seething crowd of mankind was the poor, needy woman. In all the jostling press of people, there seemed to be no one who cared for her soul. Yet there was one who knew and cared.

Could she steal a cure unnoticed by the Master? Miraculously, she somehow inched her way to His side. She reached out a trembling white hand, and the Master's robe rippled silently through her fingers. In that instant, she felt herself perfectly healed. She wanted to quietly slip away from the eyes of so many men. But the Master was not willing to let her go.

He had felt the healing virtue pass out of Him. In tenderness He asked, "Who touched my clothes?" The disciples thought this was a ridiculous question, for many crowded and pushed against the Master.

The lonely woman came with fear and trembling. She fell down before Jesus and told Him the whole truth. With great compassion, love, and kindness in His eyes, Jesus likely reached down to her, helped her up, and spoke the words that filled her heart and soul with great encouragement and joy.

"Daughter," He said with the tenderness of a Father, "be of

good comfort: thy faith hath made thee whole; go in peace."

Jesus acknowledged her healing in front of everyone. Her faith was honored, for true faith honors Christ. For this reason, Scripture records her faith as an example to all mankind. She did not seek God in vain. Though cut off from the house of God, she was not cut off from approaching Christ!

No one is beyond the reach of God's love, forgiveness, and compassion. Take heart, weary soul! You are not lost and unnoticed in the crowd. In tenderness, Jesus seeks His sheep. May you follow the example of the sick woman who. . .

· heard of Jesus.
· sought Him.
· touched His robe.
· was cured, confirmed, and comforted.

THE BLOOD OF JESUS COVERS ME

Only Jesus can meet our need for cleansing from sin, abuse, shame, and guilt. Here is an account from the life of a youth who desperately needed the help of God to function and find freedom from all her burdened past.

As my friend opened her life to God and daily walked with Him, she was amazed how that earlier confusion, turmoil, and disillusionment from having been abused was fading away. One day at work, God gave her a mind picture that helped her understand how Jesus' blood was covering her past and cleansing her life. What a freedom to realize that she was covered by the blood, and free from real or imagined guilt, shame, and pain!

There was a room; it depicted my life. On the door to the room was the inscription, "The Blood of Jesus covers me." Throwing open the door, I looked inside. Yes, here it is. I've found my load of sin and shame. I must get rid of it! Grabbing as much as I could, I turned toward the door. I staggered under the terrible and heavy load. But where could I go?

Suddenly the room is filled with a brilliant Light! Looking up, I saw Jesus standing in the doorway.

Doubt and confusion are written all over my face and fear grips my heart. Now what? What have I done? What will Jesus do?

But alas! The load in my arms is too heavy and I collapse under the weight. Exhausted, I begin to sob; sobs that come from the very depths of my soul.

The Light moves toward me, and Jesus gently removes my load and tenderly picks me up. Love is shining on His face. His eyes searchingly probe into my heart.

"My child," He says, "what are you trying to do? This was never meant for you to carry. This is only mine to cover. You can do no more. My blood had covered this. It belongs in this room. You cannot carry it out. I am responsible for this room, and I will carry your burden."

And so saying, He took my hand in His and together we closed the door behind us. The words on the door blazed brightly, "The Blood of Jesus covers me." Looking deep into my eyes, Jesus said, "The next time you wonder about any of these burdens, come to me. I will carry your sorrows."

I nodded my head in agreement. With a big sigh of relief and satisfaction, I head back to my work. My heart is light. A load is off my shoulders. I am satisfied. I know Who bore my grief and sorrows. I know what happened to them. I know it is taken care of. It is no longer my responsibility. I don't have to prove anything, as I don't have anything to prove. It is God's deal, not mine.

Signed Exodus 33:14

COMFORT IN THE CHURCH

My father passed away suddenly, unexpectedly, in August 2004. We traveled over 400 miles to his funeral. When we returned home again, six days later, I was exhausted. I wondered if my friends in Ohio cared. Most of them do not know my family. (Some of our church friends attended the viewing; that meant a great deal.)

The love and compassion I was about to experience from my church family and other friends was a "Balm of Gilead" in my time of grief. God showed His love anew to me through the sympathies His children showered on us.

I felt so weary, teary, and surrounded by work. My sister-in-law came to help me can apples and tomatoes. She ironed a big stack of shirts too before she left. Another friend helped us butcher our chickens.

We were sitting at the supper table one evening when Irene came over with a fragrant bouquet. My friend Miriam stopped in with two fresh pumpkin pies. One evening, three couples brought homemade pizza and homemade ice cream. They enjoyed the meal with us. Their children came along. That meant twenty-three children enjoying food and fun with friends and parents. Our minister and his wife showed their love and support by coming over one evening to visit. Other friends gave me a phone call.

Mark's sister, who lives two hours away, sent an attractive grocery basket through the florist. The children enjoyed all the tasty treats. Our church family taking time to reach out to us in our grief just meant so much.

When one of my friends experiences the death of a loved one, how do I respond? I hope I have learned that doing something, even a small deed, a card or a call, is better than nothing at all.

"God help me to do good, especially in my church" (Galatians 6:10). God would have us do good to all men, especially to those of the household of faith.

GIVE THE ROSES TODAY

"At my dear wife's viewing, people spoke many kind words about her. They said she was a good bishop's wife. She knew how to speak the right words," Henry Beachy shared.

"I appreciated hearing the good things about my wife, and yet I remembered how we had gone through difficult times together. Everyone has difficulties in life, in church work, or whatever. If only my wife would have heard words of appreciation in life, it would have lifted her load."

Resolve to give kind words (roses) to your friends when they are living!

KIND PEOPLE

Are we kind? Surely we who name the name of Christ should be known as people who are kind. Our hero and leader, the one we strive to imitate and to follow, was of all men the most kind and compassionate.

The Scriptures are full of accounts of Jesus healing the sick and the sinners. With kindness and compassion He reached out to touch and bless the leper, the outcast, anyone who needed love. He took time to hold and love little children.

Jesus said, "I have compassion on the multitudes." He wants us to be like Him, with a heart of love, compassion, and kindness for others.

Kindness is as a sunshine that brightens even the most dreary day. Kindness is being humane, gentle, compassionate, and tender. It is a willingness to do good, or give pleasure. It is generosity, love, and sympathy.

Over and over again, Scripture encourages us to be kind.

"Be ye kind one to another" (Eph. 4:32).

"Charity suffereth long and is kind" (I Cor. 13:4).

"Be kindly affectioned one to another with brotherly love" (Romans 12:10).

"Add to your faith...brotherly kindness" (II Peter 1:5, 7).

"Put on therefore as the elect of God...kindness" (Col. 3:12).

"In her tongue is the law of kindness" (Prov. 31:26).

After Jacob's death the brothers feared Joseph. "He comforted them, and spake kindly unto them" (Gen. 50:21). What a lovely example.

THREE MARY'S IN A ROW

It is amazing how God sends encouragement, examples, and friendliness in unexpected ways and places. I boarded the plane and chose a window seat. I was glad I could fly to Maryland to spend time with my mother; yet, I was tired and felt shrouded with a melancholy mood. It wasn't just easy to fly away from my husband and children for a number of days.

Two friendly ladies chose the seats beside me. They were laughing and talking. It looked like old friends traveling together. I was surprised when I found out they had just met that day at the Cleveland airport when our flights were delayed for hours!

"My name is Mary," I told my seatmates. They laughed.

"My name is Mary too," each of them said.

We had a pleasant time talking with each other. I told them I was flying home to spend time with my mom. They shared about their parents. We talked about middle-age health problems, and just enjoyed conversing.

The tall, chubby Mary, dressed in a black pant suit, sat by the aisle. When we took off, and whenever there was a bit of turbulence, she was scared and would grab the middle Mary's hand. The middle Mary calmly and graciously allowed the scared Mary to hold her hand. I was impressed at the middle Mary's kindness and willingness to grant the scared Mary the reassurance of care and human touch that she needed. It happened more than once!

I felt like I had learned some lessons. Why not be friendly to strangers? Why not be warm and caring? Why not brighten someone's day with the milk of kindness? Why not just be nice?

....

This chapter closes with the story of a woman of God who longed to be healthy. She yearned to be able to continue to bless the lives of her husband, children, and others. God chose to give Krystal perfect healing in His heavenly home.

God's ways often seem to be mysterious. We are unable to fathom and understand why.

Since Krystal's home going, her family has not become bitter. They are holding on to God in trust. Today they live in Thailand and minister for the Lord there.

Finding God in Pain

Krystal Dawn (Byler) Yoder
May 1, 1959 - January 7, 2006

–Delight LaDawn Yoder, age 22, May 2008

January 7, 2006, was the day my life changed forever. At the age of forty-six, my beloved mother was called Home. Unexpectedly.

She had faced death before, and after recovering from those episodes, she said, "I just want to live for my children." But it was time, and she must have rejoiced to finally enter the glorious bliss of Heaven.

As a young girl and teenager, my mom grew up with few close Mennonite girlfriends her age. Not that she didn't have friends; she just came from a small youth group and church, and lived in northern Minnesota where there weren't many Anabaptist people. Her circle of friends was primarily classmates of the Littlefork Public School, where she attended the first twelve years of formal education. To stand alone as the only Mennonite girl in a public school was hard for her, and I remember her telling me how difficult and scary it was when she first started wearing the head covering. "I was the odd one, the only person who wore the covering in this big school, and it was hard to be so different at that age."

By nature a sociable person, she made many friends, but found that the main way to find acceptance there was to be an "A" student; to make good grades. Although naturally bright, she had to work hard to stay at the top of her class. She ended up graduating as valedictorian, but this was largely due to her desperate and driving need to be perfect. Perfectionism had become a guiding theme in her life.

Coupled with this intense perfectionism, she also battled with a very sensitive conscience. In her own words, "I was a sensitive child—one of those 'super sensitive children.' Periods of my life were especially difficult as I moved from one agonizing experience of feeling I'd sinned to another. 'I didn't say that quite right. I must have lied. I should go and say I'm sorry.' Communion wasn't easy—a time of dread and fear. . . I'd talk to others about my guilt and fear, attempting to find peace and answers for the confusion that throbbed in my weary mind. It was tiresome. I had little joy. But I wanted to do what was right. Over and over, I was convicted of my sin and felt condemned. Attaining perfection as a Christian and otherwise were dominating themes of my life. I was an achiever . . . performance driven. The 'drivenness' crescendoed after marriage and children came along, and with them more and more demands."

I don't remember her struggle with perfectionism directly influencing my life—or the way she related to us children, because I never once felt pressure to be "perfect" for her, but I knew it was a tremendous source of her heart-conflict, and she often bemoaned the fact in my younger years. About her struggle with this, she writes (presumably around 1999), "Life is a journey, a pathway, a process. Change hasn't happened to me overnight, but rather in a series of one step after another. I will never forget the awesome moment when God revealed to me that I was His tabernacle and my spirit was His Holy of Holies! That at the level of my spirit I am perfect, complete, glorious, and righteous! Instead of frantically attempting to attain perfection, I am beginning to live from the basis of Perfection. There's a world of difference . . . after years of being convicted of my sin, what glory to be convicted that at the root of me I am holy and righteous!"

In 1979, at the age of twenty, and soon after graduating from college as a licensed nurse, she married my father, a pastor. As a newly married couple, they stopped in for a visit at the Sharon Mennonite Bible Institute in Pennsylvania, the school she had attended several years previously. The visit was "incidental" in their minds, but a few months later, my dad received a call from the administrator there, asking if he could come back as an instructor. This was the beginning of our family's long-term involvement with the ministry.

My oldest brother was born in the fall of 1981, and soon my mom was a busy housewife and mother. Life may have seemed perfect, but trouble brewed on the horizon. She wrote, "The year was 1984. Little did I realize that as I said, 'I love you, Dad,' and hung up the phone, that those words would be my last message to him." At the young age of fifty-four, he passed away unexpectedly during open-heart surgery. She was twenty-five. She also writes, "Just a few short months later, the Lord gave us our second healthy, contented baby boy. But one evening, I found our infant son lying cold and still on our bed. Our efforts at reviving him proved futile. The doctor's words, 'Your baby is dead,' seemed unbelievable. At the age of three months, Brendan died of SIDS (Sudden Infant Death Syndrome). A death, a birth, and another death in one year seemed overwhelming. This only happened to other people!

"Three years later, death visited us once again as a brother and a brother-in-law, both thirty-one years old, died within a month of each other. My brother had only recently arrived at New York City, the place where he had felt called to lifetime mission work. But while on his way to pass out gospel tracts, he died of heart failure."

Life went on. "In 1992, after giving birth to our sixth child, I developed viral pneumonia, which resulted in myocarditis, an infection of the heart. My heart became weakened and enlarged. Following this, our five-month-old daughter began having seizures, many of which would last over an hour, the worst climaxing in a five-hour ordeal in the fall of 1993. Many times, she was rushed to the emergency room to terminate the seizure which she could not come out of on her own. I did not completely trust God, and would taste panic and fear like I'd never known before. I never knew when I would have another emergency situation, as she had seizures about eighty-five times that year. I constantly felt helpless and out of control. I could hardly remember what it was like not to have a constant stressful awareness that at any moment I may have another trauma to deal with. I found I needed to call on God hourly to cope with the rising fear and apprehension that threatened to undo me. I began to memorize, meditate on, and illustrate many of the names of the Lord like I'd never done before. I failed the Lord many times, but He was faithfully drawing me closer and closer to Himself." She wrote this in October of 1994. Kayla, at two and a half years old, died less than a month later.

I will always remember a family devotional time we had one morning in August of 1998, four years following. We were sitting in our living room and waiting for my dad to get off the telephone so that we could proceed with our meditation. My mom was sitting across the circle from me, and with her eyes rolling back, suddenly she gasped and flailed, partially falling off the chair. The four of us younger children sat in shock and horror, then quickly attempted to get Dad's attention. She recovered on her own after ten to fifteen long seconds, but, "After hearing what happened, my doctor asked us to immediately come in to be checked over. He diagnosed my problem as being ventricular tachycardia, an abnormal heart rhythm in which the lower chambers of the heart beat so fast as to be inadequate in pumping blood to the brain and the rest of the body, thus depriving the brain of needed oxygen. It was a shock to hear the words, 'This could have been fatal. Your heart converted on its own this time, but it could very well happen again and there are no guarantees that it may not be fatal the next time. You need to surgically have a defibrillator implant put in.' The next six days were spent lying in the hospital while my heart condition was stabilized with medication. While resting there, I pondered with greater intensity than ever before the Father-heart of God."

Late one evening in January of 2004, Mom once again looked death straight in the eye. After a fun evening of animated conversation with her and my younger siblings about a weekend I'd had with friends, she came into the room the three of us girls shared and asked if we would come out to the living room. "I have something to tell you," she said. Completely unaware of anything wrong, we obeyed. "Girls, I'll be okay, but I'm having congestive heart failure right now, and I think you should take me to the clinic." My dad had left early that morning for Indiana, and my older brother was across the world in Asia, so it was up to me. And she wasn't okay. She almost died multiple times in the following weeks, and ended up being life-flighted from Johnstown, Pennsylvania, to Minneapolis, Minnesota. But she miraculously recovered, even returning to Pennsylvania approximately one month later to finish out the school year. She recovered very well, in fact. In September of 2005, she was in Minneapolis for her checkup, and we were excited to hear good reports from her doctors. They were very happy with her health, and discontinued two major drugs that she had been prescribed to take ever since the incident in 2004. "I'm feeling the best I've felt in years, if not ever!" she told one of my friends a week before her death. We truly believed she was being healed. I really didn't think about her heart condition that much anymore, because she looked so good and often said she was feeling wonderful. So on that beautiful but frigid Saturday afternoon when I heard Dad crying on the phone and with his voice breaking, say, "She's gone," I think my heart literally broke. Even now, a little over two years after her death, my heart isn't over the shock.

You see, when she died, I lost so much more than just the person who gave me birth. I lost my most trusted friend, my comforter, the one who empathized and sympathized with me so well; the one who understood me best. In the last couple years before she passed away, she told me numerous times that I was her friend, like a peer, because we understood each other so well. Almost by ritual, my younger sisters and I would gather in her room in the evenings to talk about our day. Sharing details, revisiting memories, and laughing or crying about different events was a release for us. If we didn't make it over to her room in time, many evenings she would step into our room and ask if there was anything we wanted to talk about. "Just checking..." she'd say.

The other afternoon, I sat cross-legged on the bed in my room, and with a wad of wet tissues by my side, I read through over ninety notes and cards that my mom had written to me through the years. She did so well in verbalizing and writing down her love for us, and I would often find a card from her under my pillow or propped against the alarm clock.

I truly believe that because my mom faced so many deaths and her own uncertain health, she became very intentional about living—and living well. "I will not live an unlived life," became her unspoken motto. Eternity seemed to be in reach, and this birthed an intense desire to make the most of every moment and occasion, here and now. She looked for the gold in others and loved spontaneously blessing people. I distinctly remember going through the check-out line at WalMart one day, and her telling the teenage male clerk that he had such a nice clean-cut hair-cut. At the time it slightly embarrassed me, but I won't forget her demonstration of being a blessing and face of love to those she met. One young girl in our church who didn't have many friends and often tended to be a loner was another person my mom strove to love well. This young lady was an animal lover, trained dogs, and often had competition matches at the local 4-H club. Even though it was a twenty-five-minute drive from home, and none of us particularly liked dogs, some of our family would occasionally go in and cheer this girl on because Mom wanted to be an encouraging face of Jesus to her. She passed this desire on to me because I saw firsthand the impact it made on this friend and the importance of spreading Jesus' love by making time for people and their interests.

Probably the most significant aspect of her life was her proactive pursuit of God. She embraced her pain by using it as fuel in her search to find God. Instead of passively saying, "I've had so much pain, so I hope God makes beauty out of it," she "took her turn" and ardently pursued God "right back." I often heard her say, "If you want to experience joy, you have to accept the pain in life. You cannot have joy without any pain." She allowed herself to deeply feel grief and anguish, applying and experiencing the truth of Jesus' words, "Blessed are they that mourn, for they shall be comforted." She worshiped at the Altar of Lament repeatedly. Of course, this resulted in also worshiping at the Altar of Rejoicing more because her capacity to truly live had been carved deeper by her godly reception of grief. However, her severe sorrow was not only confined to the physical losses she had experienced. I think the deaths and trials she faced before I was even born and early in my life were only the beginning of a lifelong journey of finding God in pain, because the grief I remember her experiencing the most was caused by the sin she saw and felt in her own heart. Sometime around 1999, she wrote, "I experience more sorrow and increasing joy. I am sensing to the degree I weep over the [sin] in my life that still is to be redeemed, to that degree I delight in being forgiven at the core of me. How patient God has been with me! How many years He patiently has waited at the mailbox for my return!"

Mom was such a learner—learning from anyone—older, younger, whoever, and whatever! She often shared with us the exciting truths she discovered, and taught us countless "Life Lessons" in our daily morning school sessions. I frequently remember the pictures and diagrams she drew to help us understand God and living for Him, and they've been a guiding light for me even today.

In my younger years, she would often meet with other women to give them counsel, advice, a listening ear, and prayer. I didn't resent her involvement in others' lives, because it was so obvious to us that we were more important to her. Yes, she deeply cared for the hearts of her friends, but I never doubted her first loyalty. She never made me feel like an intrusion if I came into her room and needed her attention while she was engaged in conversation with someone. In her later years, she was still involved in encouraging women and speaking at different events, but she desired and preferred staying at home. She spent hours back in her room, reading the Bible and inspirational books, praying, meditating, and writing. Her relationship with God was first priority.

I know it's sometimes easy to eulogize those who have died, or to block out the painful aspects of a relationship in hopes of proving loyal and loving, but whenever I think of my mom my mind is overloaded with good memories, and my heart almost cannot contain the joy and love I feel at the mention of her name. But everything I remember about her should bring God all the glory, since it was only because of His work in her life that she became such a godly and beautiful woman.

CHAPTER EIGHT

The Woman Who Gave

I fancy when I go to rest someone will bring to light
Some kindly word or goodly act long buried out of sight;
But, if it's all the same to you, just give to me, instead,
The bouquets while I'm living and the knocking when I'm dead.[9]
—Louis Edwin Thayer

A city on the seacoast of the Mediterranean. An ordinary house in Joppa—that is the setting for the story of Dorcas. Who is this Dorcas? Scripture records that she was a disciple. A disciple is defined as a follower of Jesus Christ. A learner. A pupil. One who studies and imitates the life of Jesus.

Known for her works of charity and compassion to the widows, she was loved by many. Widows were often the most destitute of people in those days. (A beautiful, touching eulogy to the life of Dorcas is recorded in Acts 9:36.) "This woman was full of good works and alms deeds which she did." What a testimony!

THE DEATH OF DORCAS

The sound of weeping filled the room. The widows were weeping—weeping because their dear friend Dorcas had died. Dorcas, the woman who sewed garments for them. She had helped and befriended them, the lonely widows. Now she was gone. Who would care about them now?

Dorcas had been ill. Very ill. Hearing news of her death, her friends wept and prepared her for burial. They laid her in an upstairs room.

The Christians heard news that the Apostle Peter was in the nearby town of Lydda. But wait! They had also heard the story of Aeneas, this man who had spent the last eight years in bed and had recently been healed through Peter's prayers and God's power. Many people in Lydda had turned to the Lord. Could Peter help them? They sent two men to urge him to come to Joppa with them at once.

Peter came. They led him upstairs. What a sight met his eyes, and how the weeping filled his ears! The widows showed Peter the coats and the clothing Dorcas had made for them.

"All of you leave the room," Peter requested. Left alone with the dead, Peter knelt to pray.

I wish a record of Peter's earnest prayer were ours. Scripture states only that he prayed and turned toward the body, saying, "Tabitha, arise!" The eyes which had closed in the finality of death fluttered open. She saw Peter and sat up. Peter gave her his hand, helping her to stand. Then he called for the believers and the widows, and presented to them Dorcas, alive and well!

We are left to imagine that reunion. What a time of thanksgiving God's children had. Their tears of sorrow were turned to tears of joy!

Imagine how the news raced through the streets of Joppa: Did you hear the latest? Dorcas was dead; now she is alive! Miraculous, yes, but true!! I imagine that crowds of people went to her house. Many passed by, hoping for even just a glimpse of Dorcas. For to them, seeing was believing.

I wonder if Peter spoke the same words to the people in Joppa that are recorded in Acts 4:10 and 12: "Be it known unto you all, and to all the people of Israel, that by the name of Jesus Christ of Nazareth, whom ye crucified, whom God raised from the dead, even by him doth this man [woman] stand here before you whole. There is none other name under heaven given among men, whereby we must be saved."

In the life and death of Dorcas, God was praised and many people came to know the Lord.

I wish I could know more about the life and ministry of Dorcas, but the chapter closes on her life.

I want to remember this fine lady who was known as a disciple. She was full of good works, kind things, and charitable deeds to the poor and needy around her.

Who in our lives is the most needy and destitute? May our prayer be; "Lord, what wilt thou have me to do?"

CONCERN FOR OTHERS
Dorcas was an example for us today.

"Her simple concern for others rather than powerful speech or a great singing voice won her the love of her friends and neighbors. Sometimes in our desire for a more public ministry, we forget that the greatest in God's kingdom are called to be servants, and servants are called to care for those they serve."[10]

Faithful. That word describes the life of Dorcas. What about you? What best describes your life? Revelation 2:19 and 23 tells us that God knows our works, and He will give to each of us according to our works. God wants all of His children to be involved in loving and serving.

I am challenged by the examples of women who are useful for God. One of my mom's friends sent her this letter.

I was so blessed this winter. I was able to do some voluntary service work. I went to the Galilean Children's Home in Liberty, Kentucky. I was there for seven weeks. I worked with the babies. They call it the Angel House.

We had eleven babies, all under two. The oldest was seventeen months, and the youngest was five months old. All of their moms are in prison. It is so sad. Those babies need so much love and attention.

There were three of us on a shift. All day long, we would wipe noses, change diapers, feed, love, and try to keep those babies happy.

I just want to thank the Lord for allowing me to do this kind of work. I did enjoy the babies.

I asked Edna, an elderly lady, what she does with her time. She responded, "People bring me their leftover materials. I sort out the biggest pieces to send to sewing rooms in Romania. The rest I cut up in patches to be used for quilts or comforters for the needy."

I spoke with my mother on the phone one day and was impressed with the plans for her day at age 70. She intended to visit an invalid from her church and a neighbor lady in her nineties. In the afternoon, she expected to do some cleaning at her son's house.

Savilla Glick, age 94, sews many, many dresses for earthquake victims in El Salvador, where her daughter Verda is a missionary. God bless her for reaching forth her hands to the poor and needy!

PROVOKING ONE ANOTHER TO LOVE AND GOOD WORKS

One chilly fall day, I received a thank-you card from my friend Ann. Her unique tiny script had a lot of meaning behind it. My daughter and I chuckled over the kindly contents of that refreshing note.

Hi Mary Ellen!

Randall really enjoyed himself at Matthias' party. Thanks for inviting him. It is so good for him to have other friends. The next morning we asked him about it. He told us all about it and what a good time they had, and how they surprised him, etc. And what great food you had (he loved that cake, maybe I should have the recipe sometime). I also asked him if he thanked his hostess. He said he was going to, but you all left earlier from the gym. So I suggested this card instead. You will notice he is short and to the point, writing notes and letters not being his favorite hobby.

Sure do love you! Thanks again for inviting us to the baptism and to your place. We all really enjoyed ourselves and were blessed and encouraged. —Ann

Her son's note followed:

Dear Mark and Mary Ellen,

Thank you for the invitation to Matthias' birthday party. I really enjoyed the party and the food.

Thanks again. —Randall

I read the note to our family at the supper table. We all grinned and enjoyed Ann's kind words. It also prompted me to ask my son, "Did you send a thank-you note to each one for the gifts you received? That's such a nice thing to do, you know."

Later, I inquired again. "Yes, Mom, I sent thanks to everyone!" he responded.

I do try to teach our children to say thank you when they receive a gift, and to express thanks to the host when they are at a friend's house. The example from my friend Ann reinforced in my mind the importance of expressing gratitude. It is just plain, old-fashioned good manners. Gratitude brightens up any day!

I was reminded of Hebrews 10:24: "And let us consider one another to provoke unto love and good works."

GOOD SAMARITAN IN OHIO

Years ago, Dorcas Hoover learned the Spanish language while accompanying her dad on mission trips to Guatemala. Today, though she is a busy mother, she reaches out with God's kindness to the Spanish-speaking population in her own hometown. She brightens the days for many lonely mothers and children. Dorcas shares with them compassion, clothing, and warm covers.

Dorcas relates her experiences as a Good Samaritan one dark night:

The call came last night at what Dr. Lehman always called the "perfect hour"—just before you retire and your children are tucked into bed. "I'm exhausted!" I told Jerry moments before the phone rang.

It had been a full day—church, Messiah rehearsal (no nap!), listening to a chorus program, and finally returning home at 10:30.

I could tell by the tone of her voice, that Vicenta was facing real action when she called after 11 last night. "I lost a lot of blood; I don't know why," she said, her voice strained from pain. Instantly adrenaline kicked in and the tiredness vanished. I breathed a prayer for wisdom as to whether to call an ambulance, and felt I should just rush down and check her first. I went out the door, now wide awake and refreshed after a quick snack.

After a few quick questions at Vicenta's house, I determined it would be best to quickly head for Mercy Hospital. Some of the sound effects from the seat behind me drove all sleepiness away as I thought about Dr. Lehman's roadside deliveries and wondered if I should start carrying a bulb syringe and shoelace in the cubbyhole of my van—hoping and praying I would not need them!

As we sped toward Mercy, a police guard blocked the lane to the ER while a helicopter landed on the nearby pad. The muffled noises from behind me motivated me to steer around the traffic and tell the police, who was waving at me to stop, that I had a labor patient in the van and needed to get to ER. He waved me on. I hurried into the ER. "Excuse me, ma'am," I said to the receptionist who was interviewing a heavy black man. "I have a labor patient who is in a lot of pain." We helped Vicenta into a wheelchair, and she called Maternity and requested a call for a translator.

A gentle nurse named Teresa kindly helped settle Vicenta who was at 4. I agreed to stay and help until a translator arrived. Vicenta said she wanted to go natural, and the nurse did not contest, which pleased me as I recalled other long labors I'd seen and heard of at Mercy with epidurals and then forceps and suction deliveries—perhaps to ease the translation dilemma. We chatted easily at first as she rapidly progressed and I coached her through the contractions, reminding her to breathe and relax as I gently stroked her arm. As I helped to fill out the paperwork, I thought of my first experience translating at Mercy—and my desperate prayers and searches through the English/

Spanish dictionary for appropriate words. How much more relaxed I was two and a half years later!

As we talked, I discovered she has no car seat for the baby, no name, and the father has a five-month-old baby with his American woman. The father of her first daughter, Maria, is also in Canton, and has another woman. Poor dear. When the nurse went out, I had a word of prayer for Vicenta.

Vicenta bravely endured the increasing contractions. No translator showed up, and the nurse let us do our thing, occasionally checking and once in a while reminding her how to breathe. I asked for a damp washcloth to wipe her clammy face. During those last anguished moments, I quietly whispered an occasional "Dios ayudanos!" and "Jehova es mi pastor, nada me faltara," interspersed with soothing whispering reminders for her to relax and breathe. (I'll have to memorize some more appropriate Spanish verses!)

A little over two hours after our arrival, we greeted a beautiful new baby girl—an awesome experience to witness the miracle of life once again, and then to hold the precious nameless bundle in my arms. I prayed a prayer of blessing over this beautiful new baby with a very uncertain future.

Perhaps "Ana," the name of Vicenta's grandmother, would be a good name, I suggested. But Vicenta couldn't decide and was too tired to care. After seeing mother and baby nicely settled after a snack for both, and giving last-minute translations for menus and care, I slipped out of the room—richly blessed.

How near God seemed—especially when my sluggish reactions as I turned onto I-77 at 3:45 AM caused the squealing of tires of a speeding truck who appeared out of nowhere, and with a sudden press on my gas pedal, the little van surged away from his bumper and the squealing of tires passed behind my car.

Praise the Lord! God answered my prayers in the timing of the birth—just when I was home to answer the phone—and yet wasn't needed by my family! God cares for that little nameless bundle.

Brighten Your Corner

To Ina Duley Ogdon, it seemed like a dream when she was told that she had been chosen to serve on the Chautauqua Circuit. Thrilled, she dreamed of opportunities to touch thousands of lives for God.

Shortly before she was to leave, an automobile accident seriously injured her father.

Would Ina be willing to cancel her plans to care for her invalid dad? Instead of an audience of thousands, she would have an audience of one, who would be shut up in a bedroom corner of her home. She also knew that she was the only family member available to care for her father.

At first, Ina felt great disappointment and despair, even resentment against God. Why, oh why, did her father have to be tragically injured?

Thankfully, Ina soon came to the place of quiet acceptance. God was calling her to shine her light to her father and to her neighborhood. She dared not wait for an opportunity to do great deeds. She determined to shine in her corner of the world, and God gave her a song. Her household duties became a joy as done unto Jesus. Caring for her father was a calling from the Lord!

Ina completed her poem, "Brighten the Corner," in 1913. Charles H. Gabriel set the words to a lilting melody. As though on wings, the song went out and became popular in Billy Sunday campaigns.

Only God knows how many countless millions have been blessed, challenged, and inspired by her song, for more than 25 million copies of "Brighten the Corner Where You Are" have gone out to brighten the world.

Brighten the Corner Where You Are
Do not wait until some deed of greatness you may do,
Do not wait to shed your light afar,
To the many duties ever near you now be true,
Brighten the corner where you are.

Just above are clouded skies that you may help to clear,
Let not narrow self your way debar,
Though into one heart alone may fall your song of cheer,
Brighten the corner where you are.

Here for all your talent you may surely find a need,
Here reflect the bright and morning star,
Even from your humble hand the bread of life may feed,
Brighten the corner where you are.

Brighten the corner where you are,
Brighten the corner where you are.
Someone far from harbor you may guide across the bar,
Brighten the corner where you are.

Deeds of greatness. Public ministry. Noble acts. How easy it is to aspire and to dream of doing something spectacular for God! Contrast that to serving God in a small corner. A corner sounds tiny and insignificant. Yet a corner can glow with brightness and blessing from above!

God's Word reminds us that "He that is faithful in that which is least is faithful also in much"(Luke 16:10) and "Kind deeds done, even unto the least of these, are done as unto the Lord" (Matthew 25:40).

PAPA'S ROSE IN GLORY

Mary Jane Mast was an ordinary woman who lived in Tennessee. Yet she was also extraordinary in her passion for God, her love for her husband, and her love and care for many, many children.

The little country church in Whiteville, Tennessee, was packed to capacity. There was a solemn hush. At the front of the church was Mother's casket. The song leader rose, and soon the majestic strains of Mom's favorite song, "What a Day That Will Be," filled the sanctuary.

What a Day That Will Be

There is coming a day when no heartaches shall come,
No more clouds in the sky, no more tears to dim the eye,
All is peace forevermore on that happy golden shore,
What a day, glorious day that will be,

What a day that will be when my Jesus I shall see,
And I look upon His face, the One who saved me by His grace,
When He takes me by the hand, and leads me to the Promised Land,
What a day, glorious day that will be.

The singing was wonderful and joyous. Hundreds of voices were lifted in praise to God and filled with longing for heaven. Oh yes, the family could well imagine their mother in glory. Their hearts were sad, for home without Mother could never be the same, yet they rejoiced because their mother was safely home. In the last several years, she had increasingly expressed her desire for her heavenly home. Some sweet day, they would meet again.

"Amen to that song," affirmed Bishop Eli Kauffman when he stood to preach the funeral sermon. "If that didn't make us homesick for heaven, something needs to happen in our lives. Does God do all things well? Does Jesus care? Does God really do all things well? Does Jesus really care?

"Imagine Job," Eli continued. "Everything was taken away in one day. What did this godly man do? He cried out to God and worshiped. 'The Lord gave, and the Lord hath taken away; blessed be the name of the Lord.' Those words from Job are still true for us today.

"Nearly forty-seven years ago, God gave Elmer a bride, a lover, a counselor, a confidant. The Lord gave Elmer a homemaker; that is what godly women are designed to be. They were a tremendous couple. Elmer was the head of the home. Mary Jane was the heart.

"God gave this couple five fine children. Today, Elmer and his children would stand up and call their wife and mother blessed.

"God has taken away a loving sister and friend. God has

taken away Elmer's life companion. God has taken away a loving mother. God has taken away a wonderful grandmother. Yet our Father God cares. Jesus wept at Lazarus' funeral.

"He sees our tears today. 'Precious in the sight of the Lord is the death of his saints.' God has great compassion for His children."

"Mary Jane was my best friend," sobbed a small six-year-old girl at the funeral. What a sweet eulogy to the life of Mary Jane Mast.

She had a way to make all little children feel loved. As every child is special in God's sight, so every child was special to Mary Jane. The children knew it. No wonder she was so greatly loved. No wonder so many tears were shed at her funeral.

Mom's Life, A legacy of Love
Memories shared by her daughters, Darlene and Ruby

Family mealtimes were a priority to Mom and Dad. Mother got up in time to be neatly dressed and combed. She was happy as she prepared a hearty farmer's breakfast. If I got up early enough, I would find Mom quietly reading her Bible and praying. I knew she earnestly prayed for us.

I can still just see my dad quietly sneaking up behind her chair at the breakfast table. He would say, "You look just like the first rose in springtime!" Often he would give her a fresh rose he had plucked from their garden. Then they would affectionately kiss each other. What a sweet tune with which to start out our day!

Mom was diligent and taught us girls to start our work early. She wanted us to move with a purpose and not poke. She showed us how to be brisk and energetic. She did not allow herself to become overweight or sloppy. She kept herself neat for Dad, enhancing their witness for God.

Though Mother was a good housekeeper, housework was not a top priority. She would rather have spent time ministering to people. Maybe that is why she wrote, "Serve the Lord with gladness" on her old mop bucket. On her dining room wall, she drew praying hands with the words, "Sing, Smile, Pray." She wrote expressions of praise on her dishes.

Mom was only thirty-three when she was hospitalized for thirty days. Kind neighbors cared for Davy, her newborn son, and her last baby.

Her heart would race out of control. The doctors diagnosed serious heart problems. They didn't think Mom would make it, but they had not reckoned with her faith and prayers. Mom cried out to God, "Allow me to live long enough to raise my family." God had mercy on the family. He still had a ministry for Mom.

Mom requested to be anointed with oil by the leaders of their church.

James 5:14-16: "Is any sick among you? Let him call for the elders of the church; and let them pray over him, anointing him with oil in the name of the Lord. And the prayer of faith shall save the sick, and the Lord shall raise him up; and if he have committed sins, they shall be forgiven him. Confess your faults one to another, and pray one for another, that ye may be healed. The effectual fervent prayer of a righteous man availeth much."

What a touching and meaningful service they held around her hospital bed. Confessions were made. Mom was anointed. The ministers laid their hands on her and implored God's mercy and healing if it was in His will. Dad and Mom did not know what the future held for them. They knew God was with them and His peace was real.

God graciously answered the cries and prayers of our family. Mom's life was doubled. God gave our mother thirty-three more years to live and to serve God!

MOTHER'S GODLY CHARACTERISTICS

A Dorcas Woman

She thought of others in practical ways. She collected clothing to distribute to needy people in Mexico. She fixed bags of goodies to give to poor children. When the church ladies had their monthly sewing circle, Mom loved to be there.

Mom enjoyed spending days helping a church sister do mending. Helping others put up sweet corn was a pleasure. It seemed she helped others seventy-five percent of the time. Having company for Sunday dinner was common.

A Prayer Warrior

Mom left behind stacks of prayer journals and diaries. She recorded prayers for her children and her grandchildren. She lifted friends who were struggling to God.

Most of all, she prayed for Dad. She prayed about each sermon that he preached. She prayed that he could be a godly church leader, guide the people in the right paths, and be able to make wise decisions.

A Passionate Lover of God

We often heard her singing and praising as she worked. She just loved being a child of God. She rejoiced to serve God by serving others. She poured out her life in a living sacrifice of love, service, thanksgiving, and praise. Mom loved talking about heaven. She was excited about going home. Often she would exclaim, "Won't it be wonderful when we see Jesus!"

Our parents were nearly always the first ones at church. They loved the house of God and the people of God.

A Lover of Dad

Respect and admiration to her husband was Mom's chosen lifestyle. I don't remember ever hearing Mom speak negative words about Dad. We did not hear them fuss or argue. She freely expressed appreciation for everything he did for her. Their relationship brought great security to our home. We could rest in the fact that they stood together "in love."

Time for Her Children

Mom took time to sit down to talk. She would have a snack and a drink ready when we came home from school. We loved telling her about our day.

A Caring Grandma

What fun she had teaching a granddaughter the art of sewing. They made a stack of cute doll clothes. Another day, she and three granddaughters made fascinating rag dolls. Her love was just so big; she didn't mind the mess it made. Mom was doing what she loved to do. She was a young-at-heart grandma as she jumped rope with grandchildren.

Mom's nineteenth grandchild was a Down's syndrome child. "I always thought it would be fun to have a Down's grandchild," was her response. She loved him just like the others.

Over the years, Mom coped with serious heart problems. Throbbing headaches plagued her. We could tell when she did not feel well, yet she chose to be a cheerful, thankful person.

Mom did what she could to shape and mold our lives for God. She impressed on our hearts how good and wonderful our heavenly Father is. She brought His goodness into everyday life. Like Dorcas, she saw needs and did what she could to fill them.

How wonderful it is to know that my mother, Papa's rose, is now blooming in glory. Mama is singing and praising God around the great white throne in the presence of Jesus our Savior! Oh yes, some sweet day we will meet again! "What a day, glorious day that will be!"

CHAPTER NINE

House of Hospitality

It is amazing the many ways we can serve God right at home. It is amazing how many people God sends right to our doors if we are willing to show hospitality. Lydia in this account opened her home to a minister of God, and not only that, she opened her doors to the whole church (Acts 16:13-15, Acts 16:40).

Four verses give us a glimpse into the life of Lydia.

She was . . .

· a dealer in purple cloth
· originally from the city of Thyatira
· a worshiper of God
· a woman with her heart open to God
· an attentive listener to the preaching of Paul
· baptized along with her household
· hospitable—she opened her home to Paul
· allowed believers to meet at her house

A Woman of Means

She was a wealthy merchant. Only those of wealth and high rank could afford the purple cloth she sold. It appears that her business made her a good living. In spite of her success, she sought God.

Thyatira was famous for the manufacture and use of this expensive purple dye that was difficult to produce, for it was made from the shells of the murex, an ocean mollusk.

A Worshiper of God

Lydia believed in the God of Israel, and worshiped the God of the Old Testament to the best of her knowledge. Thyatira was a great ways from Philippi. God brought Lydia to Philippi, and there she truly found God!

A Heart for God

Lydia met with other women for prayer. Apparently, there was no Jewish synagogue in Philippi. Yet there was a meeting of women, a place of prayer by the river. God led Paul to this group. God blessed these sincere seekers with a true worship experience!

Where were the men? Jewish tradition required ten men to organize a synagogue. Possibly few Jewish families lived there. Yet there at the river, Paul, with the help of the Lord, laid the foundation for the church at Philippi. In Philippians 1:1b, Paul writes "to all the saints which are at Philippi, with the bishops and deacons." In time, God did provide men to lead!

Lydia Was Attentive to Paul's Preaching

Attentive listening is the mark of a soul that hungers and thirsts for more of God. She not only heard, but was ready to obey and do. Lydia, most likely a Gentile, was the first convert to Christianity on the European continent.

She Was Baptized

Her belief in God was evidenced by her willingness to be baptized. (Mark 16:16: "He that believeth and is baptized shall be saved; but he that believeth not shall be damned.") Her baptism was an act of obedience to God.

Sharing Her Faith

She was not baptized alone. She witnessed to her entire household, which likely included relatives and servants. They too found God and chose to be baptized! Lydia's faith affected her entire household!

Lydia's Hospitality

The reference to "the house of Lydia" indicates that she may have been single or a widow. Whatever the situation, God opened her heart; in turn then, she opened her home to the servants of God. She said, "Come into my house and abide there."

Lydia's Courage

At Philippi, Paul and Silas were beaten and thrown into prison. God sent an earthquake and miraculously arranged for their release. They were asked to leave the city. First, they went to Lydia's house, and she courageously opened her doors. The believers were gathered there. Paul comforted them and then departed. What a beautiful house of prayer that must have been!

Lydia. What an honor to have her name recorded in God's Book of Life. We too can have that privilege if our sins are washed in the blood of the Lamb.

Whether we marry or remain single is a matter of our calling from God. Lydia was successful and she may have been single, a business woman. What is most important is that she was open and obedient to God. She was also generous and caring.

May we honor all godly women; those who are single by God's design, and those who are called to be wives and mothers.

Dear woman of God, do not give up and lose heart when godly leadership is lacking. Learn from the life of Lydia that women can make a difference. And like Lydia, may you too seek the Lord. Be open, attentive, and obedient to His Word. Share with others. God will provide!

JANETTE'S HOUSE

It is inspiring to peek into the house and life of Lydia. Now look into your own house. What do you see? How would you describe your house?

My sister-in-law, Janette, has a house full of warm hospitality. Her house is often filled with people. Hospitality definitely is one of her gifts!

An African Children's Choir sang at their Newberg Friends Church. Before the program, they served a meal to the choir. The main dish was a rice, chicken, and broccoli casserole. The children said they liked the rice and chicken, but some preferred to have it without the trees!

Paul and Janette opened their home to host some of the children and chaperons. They were told to not ask them about their families, because some of them had very sad and terrible happenings in their past. In spite of all that, they could sing and praise the Lord!

Janette was so blessed when she walked past the bedroom where the children were to sleep. She saw the black children kneeling by the bed. They knew how to pray. The Africans were true children of God.

One year, Paul and Janette had Chinese visitors in their house for three weeks. They hosted two fourteen-year-old foreign exchange students. Paul remarked to us that he'd never met more courteous and intelligent boys. Spiritual subjects held great interest to them.

Then too, they enjoyed hosting the Hortier family for a month. The Hortiers had sold their old home, and while the new house was being completed, they lived with my brother and his family.

When we learn to develop the gift of hospitality, we share our love and our home as God intended. Sharing with others gets our minds off ourselves, and fills our hearts with God's joy! Hospitality is worth the time and energy it takes. Hospitality is an "at-home ministry" for God!

A Friend's House

One cold winter evening, we got a call from church friends: "Would it suit you to come over to our house for homemade ice cream this evening?"

Now when someone invites our family, they are inviting eight people! Yes, we were delighted to go. We had a good evening together.

I think of Galatians 6:10: "As we have therefore opportunity, let us do good unto all men, especially unto them who are of the household of faith." It is a good thing when we invite missionaries, foreigners, and friends from out of town into our homes. Do we care enough about our church family to invite them into our house for a Sunday meal, or an evening of food and fellowship.

What do you talk about when you meet with friends at a brunch, a tea party, or Sunday school class lunch?

Let me share a little secret about brunches or luncheons that has blessed me. They are the ones when the host tells us prior to our get-together, "Bring something along to share; anything that has encouraged or challenged you lately, or something special about your walk with God."

A friend and I have the tradition of getting together at one of our houses each spring. It is a refreshing time that we anticipate.

One morning in March, Wilma Lou invited me to her house. We both have six children, love to read, and have other similar interests. Her sister Ruby, a nurse, joined us.

Wilma Lou had an attractive inviting table spread with a blue-checkered tablecloth. A candle shone its cheery welcome. She placed a juicy pink grapefruit half on each china plate. She also served a delicious egg and bacon quiche, blueberry cream cheese muffins, gourmet Ranch pretzels, and of course, coffee and tea.

Women love to get together and talk, right? There is nothing wrong with sharing about many things. Most important, though, is to have a kind tongue.

We had a great time laughing and sharing. Wilma Lou related

how a recent devotional about the song, "Brighten the Corner Where You Are," had touched her heart. She suggested we sing the first verse of that song together.

Ruby shared, "At work, there is a lot of talk and banter among the nurses and staff. Sometimes too many unkind remarks are made about a certain person. I need to be more encouraging and speak kindly. Pray for me."

I had recently been listening to a missionary tape by Otto Koning. I shared how he related when they were new missionaries in the Philippines, fellow missionaries would radio them each morning and ask how they were. Even though his wife was ill, the baby crying, and he himself feeling frustrated as he tried to heat the formula on the old temperamental stove, Otto would reply, "We're fine, just fine!" Later, he realized that he missed a great blessing because he did not share his struggles and ask them to pray for him.

"Scripture tells us to bear one another's burdens, but how can we unless we are willing to share with others and ask them for prayer?" I said. "When my mom was ill, I called some good friends and asked them to pray when I flew in to be with her. It was such a blessing to know my friends were praying. Through a difficult time, I felt a peace and assurance that I was where God wanted me to be. I bless God for friends who pray for me."

May all our get-togethers glorify God. May we be quick to speak His praises, and be an encouragement to others.

A MORNING AT MY HOUSE
The Worms That Were Left Behind

"Micah, Micah," I woke my small second grader. "Micah, it's time to get up."

"Yes, Mama," his sweet little voice answered.

I was so pleased that he was awake and happy. Last night he cried because he had to go to bed early. He wanted Markus to go to bed early, too.

This morning he was happy and pleasant. "What about the wormies, Mom? Where can I find some worms? No one else brought worms yet, and that would make my teacher happy."

I knew his teacher needed some earthworms for a science project. I didn't feel like going out and helping him dig worms. My first batch of grapes was steaming and I wanted the boys to pick off more grapes before they left. (Normally, we aren't extra busy before school, but occasionally the boys' help is greatly appreciated!)

Cheerfully, Micah plucked grapes off the stems. I told him that I'll help him look for worms after breakfast.

We went out to a flower bed. I moved a big rock. We spotted some long slender worms. Speedily, we grabbed them and dumped them in a brown paper bag. I flipped another rock and snatched a worm. "Micah, it's trying to get away from me," I called. He quickly bent to help me retrieve it. Into the bag it plopped.

We reentered the house. In my heart sprang a warm feeling that comes from taking time for my precious son's concerns and interests.

We still had time to do some more grapes. The phone rang, informing us that the school bus would not be running this evening. I forgot to send on that message till Micah reminded me. Marcellus came over to the phone to kindly help me find the next number on the list. He bumped a pan of grapes. Crash! A hundred or more grapes rolled around on the floor like marbles! The three of us soon had the mess picked up. Before long, my boys were out the door to meet the bus.

I love to watch them leave, and I breathe a prayer for my four sons as they march single file, in order of age, aboard the bus.

I went back inside and saw a small brown paper sack on the counter. My heart sank. The worms! Oh dear, the worms got left behind.

I was sad. I had so much wanted to brighten Micah's day and to send him off happily clutching a bag of wriggly critters for school.

"Oh Lord, bless his day anyway." This evening I hope to chat while I hold him. As we snuggle, maybe we can have a good talk about coping with disappointments, even small ones like forgotten worms.

The next Monday morning, we started all over again. "What about the worms, Mama? I want to take some worms along to school."

PEACE IN OUR HOUSE

We love. We laugh. We dream. We think. But sometimes the devil ensnares us in the comparison trap! We women can catch ourselves comparing our husbands with other men. Like, I wish he would cook Mother's Day dinner as a friend's husband does. Or, Ann's husband got his mother-in-law to purchase those antique dishes he knew his wife admired. Others celebrate at fancy restaurants and do big vacations on anniversaries. On and on our thoughts can run.

Instead of comparing, let's count our blessings. Here are some things I greatly appreciate about Mark. May this encourage you to focus on the many nice things about your own husband. In a silent spot, meditate on the lovely, caring things he has done. Why not take time to write down each instance, each memory?

One morning, the dirty dish water refused to leave the kitchen sink. This happened on Saturday, my day to finish the cleaning and put the house in order. That gray, greasy water in the kitchen sink just didn't agree with me.

Mark was enjoying a good Saturday morning, working in the office. I called out to him that the kitchen sink drain is not working. The water is not going down.

I think he heard a certain note in my tone of voice. In exchange of the peaceful office work environment, he went down to the basement and spent more than an hour unplugging a messy drain. Mark is a jack-of-all-trades, and we're too frugal to call a plumber. Micah, our eight-year-old, beamed sunshine into that dismal plumbing job. He cheerfully scampered out to the shop for tools, and assisted his dad in every way that he could!

I greatly appreciated that Mark left his comfortable office chair to please me, and worked on a job that needed his immediate attention. He didn't complain either. Want to hear more? I am so grateful that Mark is faithful. He makes me feel loved and pretty. He is a real gentleman. I think he loves to hold doors open for me. He provides well for his family. I like so much how he loves to sing, and that we enjoy singing with our children.

Men can do much to slay the little foxes that eat at a marriage. When he chased the dirty water down the drain, my trouble washed away too.

Plugged drains, malfunctioning wash machines, and dead lawn mowers are all little foxes. Blessed is that man who attends to what concerns his wife and keeps peace in the kitchen.

Be sure to take time to encourage your man. Tell him what you appreciate about him today.

OUR HOUSE CHURCH

On Friday and Saturday our area had fifteen to twenty inches of snow. A winter wonderland sparkled outside. On Saturday came the call that church services were canceled for the next day. After our family devotions that evening, Mark assigned some of the children a part for our own house church. Eleven-year-old Markus would lead the songs. Marcellus was to share a devotional. Matthias would talk about the Sunday school lesson. I would share an inspirational reading. We asked my mother to reminisce about her childhood, and Mark would read from the Word of God.

Sunday morning dawned clear, cold, and sunny. While the children slept I had such a precious time alone with God. At ten, we got together for worship. Each part blessed my soul. Mark read Numbers 11, and shared five lessons from that chapter. Here they are for your benefit as well.

Complaining displeases God. Phil. 2:14 tells us to do all things without murmuring. Num. 11:6: They became utterly discouraged because they focused on external things.

Gratitude dispels complaining. Complaining affects your health. Focusing on gratitude helps remove complaining. Thankfulness is the parent of all other virtues.

If it is your duty, do it! If God calls you to a work, He will provide the strength.

Complaining results in suffering. To complain is to have your focus in the wrong place.

Is God's hand waxed short? God is able to meet our needs.

Our own little church was an encouragement to me. The Sunday before, our bishop had preached a message entitled "Show Yourself a Man." He said that the greatest problem facing America is passive males. God is looking for men who will rise up and stand for truth. He searches for men who base their convictions on the Word of God and not on what everyone else does.

On a snowy Sunday, my husband took time to lead us in worship. My heart is grateful.

PALKO'S HOUSE

When I was a little girl, we had a book entitled *Sunshine Country* by Kristina Roy. I liked that story back then. Recently I read it to our small boys, and was challenged anew. It is an excellent story to read aloud, and to touch the lives of children.

This true story is of a little boy who was lost in the mountains. He was found by strangers, and taken in by kind country folk. Years later, Palko was miraculously restored to his real mother. Palko lived in a hut high in the mountains of Czechoslovakia with his benefactor, whom he called Grandfather. I will share a small part of the story to show the change that took place when Jesus came into Palko's life.

"Grandfather," Palko asked politely, "the corner where I sleep, may I consider it to be my own little house?"

"Of course," answered the grandfather. "You may call it your palace if you like."

"Many thanks, sir," said the young boy. He was well satisfied with the answer.

That night when the grandfather and the uncle returned from their work in the forest they stared in amazement at the change in Palko's corner. It was swept spotlessly clean. A large old nicked pitcher was full of beautiful fresh blossoms. Even the wall was decorated with leafy branches.

"Well, of all things," said the uncle. "You must be expecting an important guest, my boy."

"Oh yes, indeed Uncle. He has come to stay with us. I have received Christ into my house as Mary and Martha of old."

The older men smiled, but Palko's corner was such a contrast to their part of the hut that they began to put things in order, and Palko was told to sweep out the whole house!

Oh yes, when Jesus abides in our house, the world will see the difference.

ABIDE WITH ME

Who lives in your house? Who abides with you?

The word abide is used much in the Scriptures by the Apostle John, the beloved disciple. The word abide is a strong word.

It means:

· to stay in a given place, state, or relation
· to be steadfast, enduring, faithful
· to have one's abode; dwell, reside
· to continue in a relationship, and to remain attached

For the child of God, "to abide" is to remain attached to Jesus, as a vine is attached to the branch. To abide is to continue to do the will of the Father throughout life.

"Abide with me, abide with me," a dying man kept repeating. Those words made such an impression on Henry F. Lyte, the pastor who was attending his friend.

After Henry left, the words "abide with me" kept running through his mind. That evening at home he wrote a beautiful poem entitled "Abide with Me." He stuck it in a desk drawer, where it lay forgotten for many a long year.

Henry Lyte was delicate in health for much of his life. Yet he toiled on for more than twenty years as the pastor of tough seafaring men in a church on the seashore of Devonshire, England.

Pastor Henry loved to stroll by the seaside. Daily, while walking, he talked with God. There by the sea, he thought out many of his sermons. But in September of 1847, he walked with a heavy heart and uncommonly slow steps.

His physician had recently told him, "Henry, you are wearing out. You must take a trip South. The warmer climate may yet boost your health."

Henry knew that he must go. He felt his feeble frame could not endure much more.

"I must put everything in order before I leave. I have no idea how long I will be away," he mused as he packed books and sorted papers. While cleaning out a bottom desk drawer he found the poem "Abide with Me" that he had written many years before. In light of his illness and all the changes in store for him, his own poetry touched a cord in his heart.

On Sunday, September 4, 1847, Henry administered the Lord's Supper to his parishioners one last time. Tears filled many eyes as he pleaded with them to become acquainted with the changeless Christ and His death on the cross, and to prepare for that solemn hour of death which each man must face.

That evening, Henry walked down to the sea for one last time. He sat there on the rocks for a long time refining his manuscript "Abide with Me." The setting sun filled the sky with its crimson hues as he returned to his study and put the finishing touches on the finest hymn he ever wrote.

Early the next morning, he left with his family for France. His health continued to decline. On November 20, 1847, his life ebbed away.

His dying testimony was, "Oh, there is nothing terrible in death. Jesus steps down into the grave before me. I have both peace and hope."

A few lines from his own hymn "Abide with Me" are etched on his tombstone:

"Heaven's morning breaks, and earth's vain shadows flee,
In life, in death, O Lord, abide with me."
"Yea, though I walk through the valley of the shadow of death,
I will fear no evil, for thou art with me" (Psalm 23:4).

My Mother's House

My mother's house will never make it into the *Good Housekeeping* magazine. It is not fine and fancy. Yet all my children love it there, for her place is very "child friendly" and full of love.

My mother herself is the biggest attraction. She is never too busy to sit and talk. She loves children, and takes time to play Memory, checkers, or Tower Climb. Mom welcomes my children on her warm lap for a cozy story time.

There are no fancy dishes or knickknacks sitting around that little hands may not touch. But there are Tinker Toys out in plain sight, just waiting for a little person to enjoy. There is a low shelf in the corner of the living room that overflows with colorful children's books. More books are on a low table in front of the sofa. A box of Lego blocks are in a corner behind the recliner.

I sometimes envy those who live close to their mother's house. We have 450 miles to travel to my home place. At least, all our children love to go visit Grandpa and Grandma. They enjoy the old-fashioned marble roller that they can always find in the sewing room. My six-year-old remembers the magnetic letters that he can stick on the refrigerator. They like the collection of bathtub toys; boats that my brothers played with years ago.

My mother loves to read. There are stacks of books and magazines in every room. I have no fears that my children will find a book that would be an adverse influence. My mother believes in having only books that are upbuilding and edifying.

Mother loves to help children enjoy God's great outdoors. My heart is greatly warmed when I look out her window and see her walking hand in hand with my three-year-old son. They enjoy fresh air, sunshine, and the antics of frisky little lambs and kids.

She knows the value of giving a child individual attention. She kindly admired the drawings of my nine-year-old. He drew a special picture just for her. She gave him affirmation by getting him to read a story out loud. She told him, "I would like if you would write me a letter and draw a picture for me each week." The idea appealed to him.

My mother wants me to have a vacation when I come home. She loves it when I sit to read or rest. I appreciate that, but I also like to do things for her. I enjoy working in her flower beds and cleaning for her, while she is playing with and caring for my little boys.

We love and appreciate each other intensely. It tears us up at times that we live so far apart. But bless her heart, she says the most important thing is that I love God and have a faithful Christian husband. She accepts it as God's will for me to live in Ohio.

My mother's house is not fine and fancy. But it is full of what really matters—time for people, love, and care. We all feel welcome there.

Longing for "The House of the Lord"

Many years have gone by since I penned "My Mother's House." My mother's heart is gradually weakening. She is growing weary. She has a hearing aid and a pacemaker. No longer can she see so clearly.

In 2004, my dad passed away suddenly, without warning. All of the changes brought many new struggles for Mom. Now my mother is truly longing for "The House of the Lord." She is anxiously waiting for her final home. I am grateful she continues to find comfort in the Word of God and in prayer. As her body grows older, the foundation she laid years ago by accepting Christ in her life, and daily walking with Him, greatly aid her in today's trials and storms.

John 14:1-3 are a great comfort to her.

"Let not your heart be troubled: ye believe in God, believe also in me.

"In my Father's house are many mansions: if it were not so, I would have told you. I go to prepare a place for you.

"And if I go and prepare a place for you, I will come again, and receive you unto myself; that where I am, there ye may be also."

My mother's heart echoes the words of Corrie ten Boom, written while she was in solitary confinement in a Nazi prison in the 1940s.

"Once I asked to be freed, but the Lord said, 'My grace is sufficient for you.' I am continually looking at Him and trying not to be impatient. I won't be here one minute longer than God deems necessary. Pray for me that I can wait for His timing."

CHAPTER TEN

A Faithful Support

Priscilla was her husband Aquila's partner in life and ministry.

Priscilla. Her name is mentioned five times in the Scriptures. Yet her name is never mentioned alone; always, it is Aquila and Priscilla, or Priscilla and Aquila. They were a husband and wife team, united in love and loyalty to God and His work. What an example! (Acts 18:2,18,26, Romans 16:3, I Corinthians 16:19.)

Priscilla was a warmhearted woman of talent and dedication. She and Aquila were willing to enhance the ministry of the Apostle Paul by opening their home and hearts to him. Paul lived with them in Corinth for a year and a half. While they worked together in tent making, they encouraged each other and were built up in the faith. They were three dedicated, talented Christians, not ashamed of earning an honest trade by working with their hands.

Aquila and Priscilla were an effective team, intelligent in what really mattered: the things of God. Paul called them his helpers in Christ Jesus.

Priscilla and Aquila were secure in God. They did not seek the limelight in ministry; rather, they quietly supported and blessed their leaders.

They heard Apollos, a young, bold, sincere, and eloquent speaker, preaching the baptism of John in the synagogue. Aquila and Priscilla did not despise his ignorance, or ruin his reputation to others. They did not say he was not fit to preach, but quietly took him into their home and taught him the way of God and the cross of Christ more perfectly. Apollos opened himself to their kindly counsel and went on to help and encourage the believers. He convinced many Jews that Jesus is the Christ.

Their lives were not set on material gain. Expelled from their home in Rome, they were willing to leave all for the cause of Christ. Their support of Paul put their lives in danger. Persecution was no stranger. They were willing to travel and to minister in other areas. The believers met for church in their home. Wherever they lived—Rome, Corinth, or Ephesus—they were courageously committed to the cause of Christ.

Paul said of Aquila and Priscilla, "Unto whom not only I give thanks, but also all the churches of the Gentiles" (Romans 16:4b).

What if Aquila and Priscilla had not taken time to instruct Apollos? What if Priscilla had not been willing to open her home to bless others? They did not know their names would be recorded in Scriptures for an example to all generations after them. They just faithfully loved God and served.

May we, like Aquila and Priscilla, when any opportunity of serving God and our generation offers itself, take care that we do not let it slip.

TEN WAYS TO BLESS THE MAN YOU LOVE

Whatever work God has called your husband to, he needs the blessing of a supportive, virtuous woman. You can choose, like Priscilla, to enhance your husband's ministry, or you can choose to hinder him.

Consider with me, "Ten Ways to Bless the Man You Love the Most."

1. Be a woman worthy of respect

A virtuous woman is one of noble strength and character. Virtue is a result of a heart in tune with God, a daily walk with Him. Proverbs 12:4 says, "A virtuous woman is a crown to her husband, but she that maketh ashamed is as rottenness in his bones." A crown is an honor to a man. It encircles his head; he is proud of it and pleased with it.

Is your husband pleased with you? Do you encircle his life daily with your love and goodness? A man can face difficult challenges in life if he knows he has a safe haven to come home to. For want of a supportive wife, many a man cannot accomplish all God intended. A disgraceful wife is like decay in his bones, corroding his strength, tearing down everything he does.

To be a woman worthy of respect:

· Realize your need for God. He enables you to be a virtuous, godly woman, and a blessing. Don't expect your husband to meet all your needs. We must have a relationship with God to know true fulfillment and joy.

Larry Crab says that many marriages are like two ticks and no dog, both looking to receive instead of focusing on what to give.

We had neighbors who had time to relax at a campground many weekends in the summer and fall. Their children were grown. They could do what they pleased; yet, sadly, their marriage of twenty years shattered. She left, and sought comfort in the arms of another man.

We need time with our husbands. Time away from duties can be a bonus. But most of all, we need God! When I am fulfilled in Him, I can reach out and bless my husband and not be devastated when he is occasionally too busy to spend much time with me.

· Be attractive and neat. When you dated, you wanted to look your best; keep on being neat and attractive for him. Never forget that inward beauty is portrayed on your face; it is lasting. Be beautiful inside, in your heart, with the lasting charm of a gentle and quiet spirit which is so precious to God (I Peter 3:4).

· Read books that challenge and edify, instead of spending much time in fictitious stories and novels. They tend to make you unhappy in the work God has called you to. Take time to study the lives of faithful men and women of God.

2. Pray, pray, pray

"The effectual fervent prayer of a righteous man [woman] availeth much" (James 5:16).

When my little son was one, he would get so hungry when I was preparing a meal. He would toddle to the cupboard, get his little brown bowl, then hold it up to me. With pleading baby words he would beg for food. Sometimes he had to wait, but I delighted in filling his plate.

God delights to hear us pray. He delights when we come to Him. He delights in meeting our needs.

Prayer is one of the best ways to bless and help your husband. Pray:

· daily that God would give him wisdom to lead his family well
· that he would seek first God's kingdom
· for his protection from temptations
· that God would inspire him for the sermons or speeches he prepares
· that God would bless the work of his hands
· that he would have wisdom to make quick decisions
· that the joy of the Lord would be his strength

Elizabeth George says, "Each morning ask God, 'What is something I can do for my husband that would help him, cheer him, or lighten his load?'"

Pray for yourself that you would:

· truly love your husband and children. We don't always feel loving. Be committed to love.
· that you would please him. Make a dedicated attempt to please him; cook the food he likes. Respect his convictions and preferences in clothes and materials. Have time and energy for him. Kindness does come back. Sooner or later,

you get back what you give. Happy is the woman who pleases her husband.

· Pray to reverence and respect him. When a woman respects her husband, he naturally cherishes her more. Just like the valley is lower than the mountaintop, the mountain blesses the valley with streams of water flowing down.

· Pray, pray, every day.

3. Be his best support and help

"It is not good that man should be alone. I will make a help meet for him" (Genesis 2:18).

A man needs his wife to be a loving companion, a helper suited to his needs. Man was created for fellowship and companionship. Mark told me he was lonely before we were married! What a challenge to be a companion and helper!

I Peter 3:1 says, "Likewise, ye wives, be in subjection to your own husbands." I need to adapt to my own husband. I am most grateful I don't need to adapt to other men. God called Mark to be a teacher. Christian schools are a work of the Lord. He is in God's work. I need to do my best to support and bless him.

God has given you the assignment to help your husband. Study him. Learn what he needs and likes. Ask him, "Is there anything I can do for you today?"

A good marriage needs trust and tenderness. It needs respect for the work each partner is called to do. Accept your husband's position as God's plan and will for your lives.

4. Bless him with a kind tongue

"She openeth her mouth with wisdom, and in her tongue is the law of kindness" (Proverbs 31:26).

Words matter. The average person speaks twenty-five to thirty thousand words in a day. If all your words were recorded, how would your record read?

Make it a goal to tell him something you appreciate about him, something you are thankful for, each day. Men need to be respected, loved, and admired.

Encourage him with words like:

· Thank you for providing so well for me.
· Thank you for never saying, "Why did you spend so much in town today?"
· I love how you played with the children this evening.
· It's a pleasure to just sit here beside you.
· I appreciate so much how you lead out in family worship.
· I admire how you worked with the boys today.
· Be quick to say, "I'm sorry."

Angry words and sharp accusations wreck many marriages. Many a man is driven from the arms of his wife by her sharp and cruel tongue. The tongue, only three inches long, can kill a man who is six feet high. Proverbs 18:21 says, "Death and life are in the power of the tongue." Only with the help of God can you have a controlled and kind tongue.

A friend of mine related, "My life has been easier since I have adopted kind speech."

Words matter. In marriage, where there are so many words (we must talk to have a good relationship), they matter all the more. Make it a daily goal to speak kind and loving words.

5. Pleasantness and patience

"Her ways are ways of pleasantness, and all her paths are peace" (Proverbs 3:17).

This verse is referring to wisdom. Proverbs 2:6 says, "The Lord giveth wisdom." If we love the Lord and plead His wisdom, surely He can enable us to be pleasant, patient, and peaceable. To be pleasant is to be agreeable, pleasing, and enjoyable.

Whatever your husband's work is, there is likely something you wish were different. Make up your mind to fit in with his work, and what he enjoys doing.

How can you find grace to be pleasant through extra busy times? How can you be patient when some things at home take so long to get done because of all his duties? How can you support him in the work he does?

You can not do it alone. Ask God for grace and strength each day. Time alone with Him gives us strength for duties. Be understanding of the weight of your husband's responsibilities. Wait until the Lord provides time to share.

A bishop's wife shared these words of wisdom with me: "When my husband's schedule is extra busy, I try to cut back. I want to be available to bless and help him in little ways."

Stay calm. Put yourself in his shoes. Remember the Golden Rule. Acceptance of his role is the key to peace.

Focusing on the good helps so much. Praise God, my husband is a Christian. Praise God, he is busy in the work of the Lord. Praise God, he loves me and is faithful.

The epitaph on an old tombstone read: "She was the sunshine of our home." Could that be said of you?

6. Communicate and keep confidences

"Let every man be swift to hear, slow to speak, slow to wrath" (James 1:19).

Every marriage needs a high dosage of vitamin C: communication! Commit yourself to talk daily about your thoughts and feelings. Work at making time to communicate.

Sometimes, women think men should know what they want without being told. Women think so differently from men. We must learn to lovingly communicate our needs.

A wise friend of mine said, "When my husband is extra busy and I need to talk, I ask him to go on a walk with me after dinner. If I sit back and think he should know when I need to talk, it leads to disappointment."

Women love to talk. We also need to develop a listening ear, and communicate an interest in his work. Your husband may need to vent some frustrations of his day. Listen and keep it confidential. For me as a teacher's wife, I need not tell my friends how Jack is such a trial at school.

One man remarked that his wife is his favorite sounding board. "She helps me think objectively when I am too involved emotionally." To be able to give good advice and counsel, we need to be in tune with God.

It helps to be organized! Work at having the children happily tucked in bed early, to have time to share with each other before it gets so late. So many things must wait to be discussed away from the children. (Chewing school or church problems in front of the children will only help turn them away from the faith you embrace.)

Mercy's Dad was a minister. She left her parents' church for another she liked better. She said it was so nice to go to church with people without knowing about their personal struggles. How sad. Concerns and difficulties need to be kept confidential.

7. Be loyal and loving

Proverbs 31 says of the virtuous woman, "The heart of her husband doth safely trust in her. She will do him good and not evil all the days of her life."

All of us have only one life. Hopefully, only one partner; one marriage to give our best to. Why not give your husband your loving best? The choice is yours. Will you be his shining crown, encircling him with your encouraging words and loving deeds? Or will you be a burden? Will you choose to be a lazy shrew who cuts and discourages him with a sharp temper and unkind words?

Love your husband. Be his best friend. Never cut him down before others. Enjoy him. Pray for him. Nurture a loyal and loving relationship.

If you find it difficult to enjoy and love your husband, cry out to God for help. You may need help from a minister, a trusted friend, or a counselor. Get help. God can enable you to live in love and victory.

Martin Luther, a former priest, was 41 when he married Katie, 26, who used to be a nun. Luther said, "Marriage is no joke; it must be worked on, prayed over." He also said, "The greatest blessing is to have a wife to whom you may entrust your affairs."

Women often work behind the scenes, doing ordinary work for God and for the man and the family they love.

Billy Sunday, the great evangelist in the early 1900s, is said to have led approximately three hundred thousand persons to faith in Christ.

His wife Nell's influence on him was extraordinary. A woman of Scottish piety, in the time of decision, she chose the better part. She was the deciding factor in Billy's decision to abandon baseball for religious work, though that decision put their income back to one sixth of what it had been! She traveled with him in his religious campaigns, watching over his work and his personal needs. He made no important decisions without consulting her. He was a devoted husband, with complete confidence in her judgment.

"The unsung and unknown women of the earth have a large part in every achievement worthwhile. Are you among the host of women, who, like the few who followed Jesus in His earthly ministry, have served in lowly inconspicuous ways, doing small tasks from a great heart of love?"[11]

You greatly influence your husband. Give him the loyal and loving help that he needs.

8. Diligence

I Timothy 5:10 tells us to diligently follow every good work. Proverbs 27:23 says, "Be diligent to know the state of thy flocks." Deut. 6:7 tells us to teach our children diligently the words of God.

Diligence means ceaseless effort, hard work, and earnestness. A diligent wife blesses her husband in so many ways:

· By keeping the house clean and in basic order
· Preparing nutritious meals
· Teaching the children obedience, the Scriptures, and good work ethics
· Helping the children to respect their dad's time of study
· She listens, shares, and prays with the children

· She supports her husband. Seeing Mommy supportive, rather than resentful, is perhaps one of the best gifts a mother can give, even if it means carrying an extra load at times.

The children were all in bed one night when Mark came home from PTF. The next morning, he was gone when four-year-old Micah awoke. "Mama, isn't Daddy home yet?" he asked.

"Sweetie, he came home last night, but went to school already this morning. Daddy still loves you. He will be home this evening," I assured my dear little son.

The older children may say, "Dad does not have time to talk with me."

I need to communicate the needs of the family to my husband when he is not aware of what is going on. A mother is often more sensitive and tuned in to the children's needs.

A teacher has many evenings away from home; board meetings, PTFs, and other obligations. When I have good attitudes towards his duties, the children pick up on that.

We also need diligence to not neglect our children in the pursuit of other ministries. Include them when possible. I like what a minister's wife said: "We have never believed in making our children 'be examples' because Dad is a minister. What we require of them is done because we believe it's Scriptural."

9. Live the Golden Rule

"Therefore all things whatsoever ye would that men should do to you, do ye even so to them" (Matthew 7:12).

A good marriage does not come automatically. We all have to work through little foxes that irritate us. We need to learn to lovingly and kindly talk things over and improve.

One afternoon before I went to town, I called Mark at school. He asked me to get some feed for the chickens and steers. I forgot to write that on my list. I got what I wanted in town, but did not remember the feed.

I am most grateful for a kind husband! He made no big deal of my forgetfulness. He's been kind when I did something of more consequence, too, like banging up the van door on a neighbor's stone wall.

Kindness does much to bless a home. Kindness is like the oil that keeps gears running smoothly. We like when our husbands remember birthdays, anniversaries, or just leave us a special note or gift. Do we take the time to do the same for them?

Just before our sixteenth anniversary, Mark was extra busy preparing a topic for a teachers' meeting. He was gone on our anniversary. Before he left, I fixed a special supper: china, candles, and good food. I even had a gift for him. I felt sorry for myself as he drove away. We couldn't even celebrate our anniversary on the correct day. A few days later, I was pleasantly surprised when I found a big envelope in the mailbox for me from Mark. It was a lovely anniversary card. That made my day!

Later, one evening, Mark said I should come out to the porch for a surprise. The boys were grinning from ear to ear. To my delight, two big old buggy wheels that I had wanted for a long time rested against the railing. Kindness does come back! Please your spouse. He will be more apt to please you, too.

John Drescher said, "While great brilliance and intellect are to be admired, they cannot dry one tear or mend a broken spirit. Only kindness can do that."

10. Take time for sweet good-byes and warm welcomes

"Heaviness in the heart of a man maketh it stoop, but a good word maketh it glad" (Proverbs 12:25).

A loving kiss in the morning when your man leaves for work is a good habit. We never know what a day holds. I have heard it said that a man whose wife kisses him good-bye is less likely to have an accident on the way to work!

When he comes home, never meet him at the door with a stick; it's a cold, hard world, and he needs your warm, loving arms.

Do you have any sticks? Our sticks can be:
· moodiness

· impatience and irritation when he is late

· being too busy to welcome him lovingly

Mark usually calls me when he is late, and I greatly appreciate that he puts forth effort to be home by suppertime, or sooner. One evening when he wasn't home as early as usual, he came just inches from being swiped by a truck at a sharp curve on a gravel road not far from our house. I have the choice to thank God when he is safely home, or be irritated that he wasn't here sooner. Happiness is not a person with a certain set of circumstances. It is a person with a certain set of attitudes.

Your marriage can be solid and loving when it is built on Jesus and surrounded with prayer. Care enough to invest hard work and effort in your relationship. Happy homes are the product of living out the principles in the Word of God.

....

We remember Priscilla and Aquila as a dedicated team who were faithful in the work of the Lord. Those who knew Noah and Lavina Beachy remember them as a couple who were willing to make sacrifices as they endeavored to serve God wholeheartedly.

I Hear Him Calling

He heard the call in his youth: "Noah, give me your heart; I want you for my son. I love you; there will be purpose and meaning in life when you are my own!"

Noah Beachy opened wide the door of his heart. His goal and passion was to have Jesus be the Lord of his life.

Noah desired companionship. He wanted a faithful, godly wife who would bless his life. In 1949, he married Lavina Kramer. They complemented each other. Lavina blessed his life with her love and loyalty for 51 years before death parted them.

In 1961, Noah accepted the call to the ministry. Before the ordination, he had felt the call of God on his life for ministry. Now he vowed to be true and faithful for the work of the Lord in church leadership.

Eleven years later, Noah had another call. "Noah, would you be willing to serve on the board for the mission work of AMA (Amish Mennonite Aid)? After much prayer and soul-searching, his answer was yes. He served with AMA for 25 years. He was their secretary treasurer for 20 of those years.

The mission board asked Noah and Lavina if they would be willing to teach Bible school in Belize and visit El Salvador in the winter of 1972-73.

What a challenge it was to teach the energetic black children in the warm, tropical climate of Belize. This was a worthwhile experience, equipping the couple with an understanding of the mission functions and helping them to identify with the experiences of the many new missionaries they helped to recruit.

They never forgot that first trip to El Salvador. They could not speak Spanish and felt like strangers indeed, but managed to get a taxi and gave the driver the address of the mission in San Salvador. The taxi driver could not find the mission, as the numbers on their paper did not match the street number. They drove around and around in circles. Lavina felt frustrated. "Whatever will happen to us?" she wondered. Finally, they just stopped. They were amazed when they saw an American man they knew by the roadside. It was Mervin Lapp! He was trying to start his vehicle by pushing it along the street. Happily, he took Noah and Lavina to the mission. Lavina felt God had stopped his vehicle at just the right time.

Life was full and busy for Noah and Lavina. Nearly every year, they took a trip to visit the missionaries in Belize and El Salvador, providing valuable support and advice for them. Noah liked it best when Lavina went along, but they also knew on occasion it was better for their family if she stayed at home. Their six children supported the mission work, yet their parents knew there was no greater mission than their own family. All their children love the Lord. Lavina says it is in spite of them, not because of them.

Lavina loved children. When their oldest daughter was in her teens, Lavina had the desire to reach out and help some poor child. To her joy and amazement, Noah brought up the subject one day. "Why don't we consider adoption, Lavina? We have enough to care for another child." Lavina agreed. She was at home anyway, so why not? The couple prayed fervently about the matter. Lavina knew Noah had a great heart of sympathy for the less than fortunate, the shy, lonely, and handicapped. Gratefully, she understood that her husband's goal was not material gain; he wanted to do what he could to bless and aid his fellowman.

Local adoption did not work out. They talked many times with Paul Eichorns, who had adopted children from Korea. They were told that there were many Korean girls who could not care for their babies who were fathered by American men during the war. Their desire to love and care for one of these children grew.

Then one day came the unforgettable call: "We have a little Korean boy for you!"

August 1968 found Noah and Lavina at the airport in Chicago. Excitedly, they watched the large jetliner circle and land. In that plane was a dear little two-year-old Korean boy, Johnny Moon. He needed Christian parents who would lovingly care for him and guide his footsteps. Eagerly, they took little Johnny in their arms.

In December 1970, they came to Chicago again, with open arms for Grace, another infant from Korea. Today Lavina testifies, "These children have been a real blessing to us."

When Noah and Lavina reached their early seventies, you would think they would have been ready to retire and relax in a warm climate somewhere. Noah was plagued with arthritis. Then the call came, "We need a couple to help with preaching and mission work in Africa."

Should they answer this call? As always, they prayed much before answering. In 1997, they boarded a plane, bound for more kingdom work. They helped out for nine months. Noah remarked, "If we ever retire, let's move to Kenya. Arthritis doesn't bother me here."

At the mission compound one day, an excited man came and urgently wanted Lavina to come attend his wife. Lavina went and was at loss what to do. Finally, they took the woman to the doctor and then to the hospital, where a baby boy was born. They had to take the lady her meals every day she was in the hospital. The little one was named Noah! Noah has more than one namesake in Kenya.

May, June, and July of 2000 found them working for God in Africa again. This was Noah's last mission trip, the last call for service in a foreign land.

Why does God call some of His children to walk through the valley of sickness and suffering? Who can understand the ways of God? Noah's health began to fail. In October 2000, doctors diagnosed him with cancer.

Through his days of illness, the Lord and His wonderful words of life were more dear and precious to Noah than ever before. God was with him through this valley of the shadow of death. Noah found comfort in the words of II Timothy 4:6-9:

I am now ready to be offered,
The time of my departure is at hand.
I have fought a good fight,
I have finished my course,
I have kept the faith:
Henceforth there is laid up for me a crown of righteousness,
Which the Lord, the righteous judge, shall give me at that day:
And not to me only, but unto all them also that love his appearing.

On May 27, 2001, God gave Noah a final call—the best yet— the call to come home to Him in glory. Noah's son, Lonnie, read Psalm 73 to his father on that morning. He asked if he was about to experience a new dimension. Noah smiled his familiar broad smile and said, "I can hear Him calling my name."

His wife and children sang old familiar hymns of comfort and hope around his bedside. They recited Psalm 23. Noah could still mouth the words. They had a blessed time of saying farewell. That night, Noah answered God's call to come home.

"Jesus is Lord" is the fitting inscription on Noah's tombstone.

Noah and Lavina had been married 51 years. How does a woman cope through all the changes that death brings? The adjustments were difficult, but Lavina testifies that God's grace is sufficient. The same God that led *them*, now faithfully continues to lead *her*.

Lavina still has a heart for foreign missions. Nearly three years after her husband's death, at the age of 76, she plans to travel to Romania to help her daughter and her husband, Lee and Celesta Gingerich, and their sons. Celesta is in charge of a guest house and is a busy lady, caring for the guests, cooking for crowds, and gardening. She will gratefully welcome her mother's help.

God still calls His children to love and service. Lavina's goal is to be faithful to that call.

CHAPTER ELEVEN

The Influence of Faith

Many mothers of famous Bible characters are not named in the Scriptures. Who was King David's mother? Who was the woman who influenced Queen Esther for God when she was young? Who was Prophet Elijah's mother? Whatever their names, whoever they were, it is most probable that they diligently taught the words and ways of God.

Lois and Eunice were a mother and daughter team, remembered for their sincere and genuine faith. Their deep faith in God was free from hypocrisy and pretense. Their lives and faith impacted the next generation for the cause of Christ. The apostle Paul lauded them for their faith!

"When I call to remembrance the unfeigned faith that is in thee, which dwelt first in thy grandmother Lois and thy mother Eunice, and I am persuaded that in thee also" (II Timothy 1:5).

Acts 16:1 says that Timothy was a disciple, the son of a Jewish woman, a believer, but his father was a Greek.

Some Bible scholars feel that the silence regarding Timothy's father suggests that he was not a convert to Judaism, nor a believer in Christ.

To a staunch Jewish family, it was a great disappointment if their daughters married outside their faith. Had Eunice greatly devastated her mother in her youth?

By the time these Scriptures were written, both women may have been widows. At any rate, any child born of a forbidden marriage was not allowed to enter the assembly of the Lord. Because of this law or custom, Timothy could not enroll in the synagogue or to Jewish schools. A half-breed, an outcast to the devout Jews: these phrases describe Timothy's reputation.

Where did he acquire his knowledge of God? Somehow, Lois and Eunice made the best out of a difficult situation. We admire their consecration and commitment, their teaching and training Timothy in the Word of God.

"And that from a child thou hast known the holy scriptures, which are able to make thee wise unto salvation through faith which is in Christ Jesus" (II Timothy 3:15).

Timothy was taught the Holy Scriptures. "That from a child" means from infancy, from very young. He learned of God on his mother's knee.

The oldest university was not on India's strand,
Nor in the valley of the Nile, nor on Arabia's sand;
From time's beginning it has taught and still it teaches free
Its learning mild to every child—the school of Mother's Knee.

The oldest school to teach the law, and teach it deeply, too,
Dividing what should not be done from what each one should do,
Was not in Rome, nor Ispahan, nor by the Euxine Sea;
But held its sway ere history's day—the school of Mother's
    Knee.

The oldest seminary, where theology was taught,
Where love to God, and reverent prayer, and the Eternal ought
Were deep impressed on youthful hearts in pure sincerity,
Came down to the earth with Abel's birth—the school of
    Mother's Knee.

The oldest, and the newest too, it still maintains its place,
And from its classes, ever full, it graduates the race.
Without its teaching, where would all the best of living be?
'Twas planned by heaven this earth to leaven—the school of
   Mother's Knee.[12]

—Author Unknown

Mothers and grandmothers wield so great an influence. Lois, of course, did not state, "Follow my godly example so that our names will be recorded in Scriptures for people to read two thousand years later!" She was just doing deeds that grandmothers do when they are committed to doing what God wants them to do in little things.

II Timothy 1:5 is also the only time in Scripture that we find the word grandmother. Lois had a heart of love to God, a love for His Word, and a love for His will. Her sincere love and faith wonderfully influenced her daughter Eunice and her grandson Timothy.

Lois' name means agreeable, Eunice means good victory. Lois and Eunice agreed together to do their utmost to teach Timothy for God, and God gave them victory!

SOWING SEEDS

Working with our precious children is the best and most important kind of gardening we can do. What greater challenge could parents have than to teach God's timeless truths to tender young lives?

Someone cried, "Where must the seed be sown
To bring forth the most fruit when it is grown?
The Master heard as He said and smiled,
"Go plant it for me in the heart of a child."

—Unknown

What do you plant in the minds of your children each day?

Plant seeds for God. Take time to discuss real things about God with your children. Learn Scriptures together, sing, talk about the Lord, and pray.

The key to passing on the vitality of our faith is to take advantage of the teachable moments in the daily classrooms of life: mealtime, playtime, work time, bedtime. Take advantage of these golden moments when little minds are most impressionable for God!

Mealtime Scriptures: Friends of ours read a chapter or more from the Word of God each morning. I love it when we recite Scriptures together at the breakfast table. A portion typed out and posted on the wall makes this easy and convenient. Scriptures and songs in the morning help to fill the mind with God throughout the day. I feel blessed when, later in the day, I hear the children singing the very same song we sang in the morning.

My twelve-year-old son grumbled one evening when I told him it's time to do his Sunday school lesson. A Scripture verse popped into my mind and I had him repeat after me, "Wherewithal shall a young man cleanse his way? By taking heed thereto according to thy word" (Psalm 119:9).

"And these words which I command thee this day, shall be in thine heart. And thou shalt teach them diligently unto thy children, and shalt talk of them when thou sittest in thine house, and when thou walkest by the way, and when thou liest down, and when thou risest up" (Deut. 6:6-7).

It is imperative for parents to make the most of their godly influence before the rest of the world gets a chance.

· Teach children from the Word of God.
· When problems arise, go to the Word for answers and solutions.
· In disciplining, go and explain from the Word why it is wrong. Your child needs to learn to fear and respect the Word of God.

—from a sermon by Roman Mullet

Two Things That Teach Wisdom

Scripture specifically makes mention of two things that will teach our children wisdom:

First is knowing the Holy Scriptures (II Timothy 3:15).

Secondly is the rod and reproof (Proverbs 29:15).

Knowing the Scriptures

It is just amazing how fast a small child can memorize Scriptures! When our children were infants, I would often quote Psalm 23 while changing their diaper. When they were preschoolers, I tried to work on a short passage with them each month. Having a copy of the verses on the wall by our table helped me to remember to practice their verses. Before or after lunch was a wonderful time to recite Psalm 8, Psalm 100, John 14:1-4, or whatever else we were working on.

When we went to town, or basically whenever we went away, we would practice our verses. I found that keeping a list of verses by their bed was a good reminder to recite Scripture at bedtime.

All children love when their parents linger at their bedside! Loving them and loving God's Word together is a wonderful blessing!

One evening, the speaker at church quoted one of the passages we had recently memorized. Micah turned to look at me, beaming with smiles. I loved smiling back at him! Memorization enabled the sermon to make more of an impact on my son.

Here a little, there a little, we shall learn God's Holy Book!

Our homes are filled with so many books. Colorful, fascinating books, all shapes and sizes. My small children loved when I read to them. I loved when I had a schedule. Right after lunch was our time to sit down and read only Bible stories. With some of the children that time was in the morning. They knew it was our Bible story time, and they weren't begging for other books. Oh yes, we liked that cozy time, the youngest on my lap, the others cuddled against me. If we knew a chorus that went with the story, we enjoyed singing it.

One day, I read out of *The Bible in Pictures for Little Eyes*. Micah was looking at the picture of Jesus' baptism, where Jesus and John were in the water. I told him that in our church, the bishop pours water on the head.

"No, Mom," he piped up, "they put their feet in water, too."

Bless his heart, he was thinking of our practice of washing the saints' feet. I told him that his sister plans to be baptized this summer.

"Why, Mom?" was his response.

"She loves the Lord and wants to do what is right," I assured him.

Oh, those golden teachable moments!

The rod and reproof give wisdom

It does not take long to see and realize that our darling baby has inherited the sin nature. Taking the time to teach our children obedience at a tender young age is of utmost importance. Often, it may seem the easiest to just turn away and not notice. We must care about what is happening in their days, and not leave them to themselves.

We need to remember God's Word, "A child left to himself bringeth his mother to shame"(Proverbs 29:15). We must take time to teach obedience.

One busy morning, my small son threw his vitamins down on the kitchen floor. I instructed him to put them back up on his high chair. He would not. I put him over my knee and gave him some whacks with a big stirring spoon. Again, I told him to pick up the vitamins, but he would not. I spanked him again. Although it was not a hard spanking, he got the message. Praise God. He then obeyed and had a happy morning.

Another day, I was anticipating a morning tea at nine with some church friends and a new lady who was attending our church. We wanted to get better acquainted and to be an encouragement to her.

When my morning work of washing the dishes and tidying the house was done, I sat down to nurse my baby dear.

I called to my three-year-old. "Put your pajamas away, and put your sandals on." I was shocked at the defiant look and emphatic "no" which he gave me.

I sighed wearily and said, "I will spank you if you do not obey." (Mothers need to remember that deliberate disobedience needs to be attended to.)

When my baby had his tummy full, I spanked my small, stubborn son. Oh, I was grateful he obeyed with just one spanking.

"Father God, I stretch my hands to Thee for wisdom and strength."

I want to remember that the most important calling for many women is the calling to be a mother—a God-fearing mother. Yet sadly, people often look down on full-time mothering in the world today.

You are too busy if you don't have time to:
· Be quiet alone with God.
· Cook delicious meals.
· Keep the house clean and tidy.
· Enjoy your children.
· Read to them.
· Make your home a haven.

One of our goals in mothering should be to live a joyful, godly life so that our children have an example worthy and attractive to follow. It has been said that our example speaks louder than our words. Can we say, "Follow me as I follow Christ?"

I loved Alta Beiler's testimony of how her parents, Crist and Rachel, impacted their children's lives.

She shared, "My parents taught us the importance of tithing. They very readily gave of their money to the needy, to missionaries, and to needs in the church. They also taught us the importance of respect and obedience to any authority, and especially to our church leaders. When there were church activities, they were there, and it was important to them that their children were there, too.

"Promptness was ingrained in us. Never show up late for any commitment you make; it steals other people's time. Someone asked my dad how he can always be on time at work. He commented, 'It is as easy to be on time as it is to be late. It is a mind-set.'

"My mother was very involved at our church sewing circle. All other work and activities were laid aside that day to attend early and stay till it was over. Dad was very supportive of her in this, and I can just see him put money in her hand that morning to put in the offering plate."

Broken Toys and Bus Behavior

While our family was in Oregon visiting my brother, friends of ours stayed at our house. When we returned I found this note and eight quarters on my sewing machine.

My boys, Carlin and Wesley, are very sorry that this toy broke while they were playing with it. They were supposed to be going to sleep and I think there was some grabbing involved. The details are a little unclear to me...however, my boys want to and need to take responsibility for what happened. They apologize and want to pay for a replacement.

There are so many things for parents to attend to and work with their children. We need to care about what is happening in their days, and not leave them to themselves.

One day, one of our little boys brought a note from a friend home from school. It read, "I am sorry I pinched you."

We were working with him about better behavior on the school bus. Things like no hitting and stay sitting. I had helped him trace his hand on a paper, and then wrote the words, "Lord, help my hands to be kind." We hung this by his bed.

I had also spoken with the mother of his seatmate about the turbulence on the bus. We both knew our sons were unruly, and wanted to do what we could to help them.

That small note from his friend spoke to his heart. My son wanted to write a note of apology, too.

Bouquets from Boys

I looked up the dictionary definition for the word bouquet. It was the second definition that surprised me.

1. a bunch of flowers. 2. a compliment.

Bouquets brighten up the day!
I am very delighted when I
Receive either kind of bouquets,
For all mothers get weary in the fray.

I appreciate my mom and here's why:
1. Whenever I need something, she'll see it and take care of it.
2. If I have a problem with my homework she'll make time to help me.
3. If I have a problem in my life, she'll help me with it.
4. She always encourages me.
5. She takes time to help us children play Three Dollars.
6. She doesn't get angry at me.
7. She likes me, or tries to.
8. She's not always so stingy.
9. She always tries to get me to finish my homework.
10. She's the best cook in Holmes County.

—Friedrich Miller, 8th Grade

I appreciate my mom and here's why:
I love my mom's food, there is not a better cook in the world. My mom is very pretty, and she puts up with me. She spends time with me, and shares my sorrows and joys. She shares my interests, like I love animals, so if my hen has chicks she wants to see them, and she likes the dogs. I couldn't have asked for a better mom. I don't know what I would do without you, Mom.

—Marcellus Beachy, 8th Grade

I wouldn't want to do without my mom:

1. I would go hungry a lot if she weren't there.
2. She gives our place an atmosphere of care.
3. I would run out of things to wear.
4. When I need encouragement she is there.
5. She helps me with my schoolwork if she can.

—Matthias Beachy, 9th Grade

Bouquets from Girls Are Just as Special!

I appreciate my mom and here is why:

My mom does a lot of things for me like washing my clothes, signing homework slips. She also taught me the Bible as I was growing up, and is still doing that today. Another thing that my mom does that I appreciate is she makes me get all my things finished and helps me get my work accomplished in time. I really appreciate my mom.

—Lori Miller, 8th Grade

My mom is the best mom anyone could have. She is always cheerful no matter how tired she is. She is always looking on the bright side of life, never have I heard her complain about the weather or the trials she faces. It is fun to work with her because she thinks of ways to do it so it will be more fun. She also cares for us deeply. Whenever we come home from school, she always asks us how our day was. Altogether, I think my mom is one of the best examples to follow for my life.

—Stephanie Wengard, 7th Grade

May we strive to give each one of our children the proper love, care, and attention that they need! May God help us to make our homes a joyful place where our children find a true haven, a place of love and acceptance. May God help us to teach our children from the most important book, the precious Holy Word of God.

"The world with all its glory shall pass away; the hills shall melt, the heavens be wrapped together as a scroll, and the sun shall cease to shine; but the spirit that dwells in those little children whom you love so well shall outlive them all and whether in happiness or misery will depend much on you.

"The time is short, the fashion of this world passeth away. He that has trained his children for heaven and God rather than for earth and man, he is that parent that will be called wise at the last."

–Source Unknown

. . . .

The apostle Paul was an encourager. He called Timothy his own dearly beloved son. To others he said, "We give thanks always to God for you all."

Here a mother-in-law gives thanks that her grandchildren are being taught the good things of the Lord. Her heart overflows with gratitude that her son and daughter-in-law, like Lois and Eunice, do what they can to impact their children for God.

WHY I THANK GOD FOR MY DAUGHTER–IN–LAW

—Ann Yoder

May this be inspiring, encouraging, and helpful to know that there can be wonderful relationships with in-laws. My daughter-in-law is a real Jewel in more than one way!

On our refrigerator, with pictures of the grandchildren, I keep this saying, "I'm not rich and famous, but I have priceless grandchildren."

Jewel is an answer to prayer; I have prayed for our children's future spouses ever since our children were young. When our son got married, I told his wife that I realize I will never again have the same place in Eugene's life. She is now the lady in his life and I am grateful that I feel comfortable with that. I assured her that I would continue to pray and support her as she became part of our family.

When Eugene and Jewel's first child was born, I sewed a dress for her. The next time they visited us, Jewel returned the dress and explained that the fabric was fancier than people wear in their church. I appreciate her loyalty to their church and obedience to her conscience. I still value her sensitivity. While it is neat to discover that we have many of the same values, it is also interesting to hear some different ideas from someone who did not grow up in our home. Jewel thinks things through and articulates her thoughts well. I appreciate the way she wants to continue learning.

I see five loves in Jewel's life that are very important to me: her love for God, her husband, her six children, her in-laws, and those beyond their own home.

Her love for God: To be a Christian, one must learn to seek God on a daily basis. Jewel does this in numerous ways. She makes time to read the Bible and pray. She is willing to teach the ladies and youth girls' Sunday school classes. She realizes that God speaks through His Word. Her desire to know God's Word will "guide her in all truth." Her private world is so filled with God's love that it flows out to those around her.

Her love for her husband: I appreciate how she cares for Eugene. She helps him grow by dreaming with him, as well as working with him. She edits his writings, decorates his schoolroom, and affirms his decisions with the children. She plans for time alone with him, realizing it is needful for continued strong connection. She speaks well of him.

Her love for their six children: Jewel says, "Reading good books, singing good songs, and Scripture memorization are ways I try to impact my children for God."

She recommends reading worthwhile missionary stories and teaching the wonders of God's creation through good books. Sometimes they have a hymn for the month. It has made singing in church more meaningful for their children. They value memorization so much that summertime finds them learning more of God's Word. One school year they memorized the book of James.

I am especially grateful that Jewel prays a lot with her children.

Bringing small concerns and losses to God helps children be God conscious and aware of His love and power. I will share some of Jewel's thoughts on teaching children to pray.

"Our oldest child was about two when I realized she did not hear many personal prayers. We pray at mealtimes, say the Lord's prayer, recite a bedtime prayer, pray in church, but what about the kind of prayer when I pour out my heart to God and ask for specific needs? My personal prayer time and prayer over a sick child were usually silent. I made a decision to start praying out loud.

"'I love You, God. I want to obey You. I know You see me when I do things,' my three-year-old son prayed. It was one of his first spontaneous prayers that came from his heart without me coaching him. It was a special moment. (Earlier that day this same child had said to me, 'I don't need to obey you, and that's the truth').What an opportunity to open God's Word and show him the real truth!

"One day at naptime my daughter's special toy was missing. I thought of my decision. We prayed out loud together. We soon found that toy. She settled down in her crib with a smile, happy in her trust of a God that is good.

"As a little child my daughter was seldom afraid. As she grew older there were times she was scared at night. Many times I prayed with her. Later I began to tell her to talk to God herself and to recite verses. She has a vivid imagination and could lie awake thinking of many scary things. Talking to God and reciting Scripture passages helps her focus on the right things and alleviates fear.

"I try to teach reverence during times of public prayer. I want to teach my children to pray with their eyes closed. Mothers need to know what their children are doing during prayer. I have noticed children looking around during prayer, bothering a sibling, whispering to a friend, or playing with toys while Mom and the rest of the church were praying. I must teach my children and not simply assume they will be good.

"God has answered prayer after prayer for us. I could tell you of the puppy who was smothered by her mother. My daughter and I cried, prayed, and worked over the puppy and she began to breathe again. Another time we tried and tried to start the tiller. We finally prayed and the tiller roared to life. The children were missing a certain special Lego. We prayed and God showed us where it was. Why has God so miraculously answered many of our children's prayers? Often His answer to me is to be patient and wait or a simple 'no,' but my children get many instant answers. I feel God has chosen to beautifully show my young children that He is alive. He is powerful. He wants to be involved in the details of their lives."

Children catch what is in their mother's heart rather than just her words. Jewel has a goal to be cheerful and content. She deeply desires that for her children too and so they have a thankful jar.

One Sunday in church the sermon was about the Israelites and all their terrible murmuring. God was displeased. The next day Jewel was not happy with all the complaining she heard in their house—*the food was not good, there was too much work*...She decided that for every complaint she heard, her child must say, GOD HATES COMPLAINING, five times, and loud enough for everyone to hear.

Later she carefully taped two neatly typed lines on a jar— GOD HATES COMPLAINING and IN EVERYTHING GIVE THANKS. On a day when the children have the grumbling bug the jar comes out, and for each complaint they drop a token in the jar and state, "God hates complaining."

Her love for her in-laws: Coming to our house is very special to Jewel. She respects our unique ways and is okay with things we naturally do differently. I enjoy giving candy and gifts to our grandchildren, and Jewel feels all right about that. She is also great at expressing thanks and appreciation for gifts given to her, and finds creative ways to use them. I often tell her that if she cannot use a gift I give them, she should give it to someone who needs or wants it. I have heard her say that if she and Eugene would fight, she believes I would stick up for her. And I think maybe I would!

Her love for those beyond their home: Not only does she love her own children, but she also loves other children. She reaches out to Eugene's school students by noticing and talking with them both in and out of school. Once a year, she plans a slumber party with the school girls while the boys go hiking with Eugene. She includes interesting, but serious, spiritual talks with them. Only God knows what these seeds may accomplish in their lives. Another way she reaches girls is by being willing to talk with them anytime. She loves the neighbors' children, and takes time to invite them into their home. Finally, she loves babies. They are all very special and important.

I have learned a lot from her example of hospitality. Even with their family of young children, she is quick to invite strangers or family. She takes time to learn to know people better. Much of that is done in their home, around the dinner table. She has decided that people are more important than extravagant meals and is comfortable with the simple and basic. She often invited young people to eat with them when Eugene was in teachers' training at Faith Builders. It was special for the youth to eat with a family.

Mothers need a sense of humor and the ability to laugh. I like the funny little children's stories she shares with us.

One day when the baby was fussy and not feeling well, Jewel decided to give her a bath to try to help the situation. Their two-year-old came in and said, "I'm grumpy, too. Can I take a bath?"

Wendall did not want to go to Sunday school class when he turned four because he was afraid he could not find them afterwards. Jewel told him they would find him, because she never yet lost any of her children. He said, "How do you know?"

One year, at Jewel's suggestion, they decided to go on a shopping fast for the month of January. She said it was time to eat out of the freezer more, and catch up on the food that is in the cupboards. After six weeks of not going to a grocery store, they had used up a lot of those things that get pushed to the back of the cupboard. It was a challenge to keep good meals on the table when some of the basics like potatoes and rice were used up. She concludes that the best way to save money is to not go shopping. I like her creative ideas for being thrifty.

"Mothering has done a lot in keeping me from being selfish," Jewel tells me. I appreciate how she loves and takes time for her children. She has slumber parties with them when Eugene is away overnight. They all settle down in one room and enjoy each other.

I am grateful she creatively teaches and trains their children. She excels at finding work for them. The old house they live in takes a lot of hard work to keep clean. They enjoy a garden and like eating healthy. Her children are right there helping her with canning and baking. They grind their own wheat for whole wheat bread. They often skim their "farm milk." Then the children make butter with the cream by shaking it in a quart jar till butter appears.

When the children are bored or disagreeable she says they need more work. That piece of wisdom makes them more ready to play nicely. However, she also plays with them, doing things like building snowmen or sledding. As a family, they like going on walks. They notice the different flowers along the way and have learned the names of many of them. Jewel helped Melanie make a book with the flowers (after they dried them), adding the name of each one.

I praise God for her consistent attitude of gratitude! Once she said she was just thinking about how refreshing grateful people are, and is asking God to make her that kind of person.

Most of all I praise God that Jewel does what she can to teach her children for God.

"And that from a child thou hast known the holy scriptures, which are able to make thee wise unto salvation through faith which is in Christ Jesus" (II Timothy 3:15).

CHAPTER TWELVE

The Queen of His Heart

Through a strange twist of events, Esther, a fine Jewish maiden, became the queen of a pagan king. Through many difficult days I believe Esther held on to her faith in God.

Esther was a royal queen. King Ahasuerus, her husband, was left with vast wealth and a luxurious palace handed down from his father. Historians describe him as a cruel, impulsive, unpredictable, and sensual man.

Did Esther have any choice in the matter? Whether she liked it or not, she was a queen to an ungodly king. She could choose her attitude though. And it appears that she had a sweet, sensitive spirit and related kindly to others.

Esther shared the king's love and attention with hundreds of other women. Poor Esther. The kings of those days seemingly had no concept of the beauty of God's plan of one man and one woman for all of life.

Esther was no stranger to loneliness. She could not freely talk to Ahasuerus whenever she wished without risking her life! There could be a lapse of thirty days or longer that she would not even see or speak to him. The royal palace was little better than a royal prison. So strictly did the laws of Persia confine the queen. The only way to confer with her uncle Mordecai was through her attendant, Hatach.

Yet Esther had influence and was mightily used by God to save His people and hers. She is remembered as a woman of courage. A beautiful woman who did what she could for God.

What happened to Esther in later years? We can speculate that as a queen she may have lived far into the reign of her stepson Artaxerxes. She may have been a person of influence in the days of Ezra and Nehemiah.

Esther Attributes

What can we learn from the life of the lovely Queen Esther?

She was beautiful and of a lovely character

Esther was without a doubt a beautiful woman. She also possessed an inward beauty that enhanced her physical beauty. Her greatest beauty was her wisdom and virtue.

What about you? Your husband thought you were beautiful on your wedding day. Are you still attractive to him? Most of all, and of utmost importance, how is your inward beauty?

God is calling us to love Him first with all our heart, and realize that He is the one who truly satisfies. Only as our needs are met first in God can we truly bless and help our husband. The ultimate in life is not about a wife or a husband; it is about a love affair with God!

An ideal marriage is a love triangle, in one corner the wife, in the other the husband. At the apex of the triangle is God Himself. The more we love and abide with God, the closer we are to each other.

Don't neglect your quiet moments of waiting on God. If you do, you will not have the quiet and peaceable spirit with which God wants you to bless your home.

It definitely helps a mother's frame of mind to have a quiet time in the afternoon. A friend who home schools shared with me, "All my children are required to be quiet for half an hour. I read, have a devotional, or a little nap. This helps me to cultivate cheerfulness. The payoff for being cheerful is much better than if you are a grump. Who likes to live with a grump? No one, not even yourself!"

When you vowed those wedding vows you made the solemn promise before God and man to "live with him in peace, as long as you both shall live."

Vows are not a light thing. They are an expression of your will, choice, and promise. Sixty percent of marriages end in divorce. Don't adapt to your culture. Build on solid biblical convictions. Marriage is for life. You can be a helpmeet if you live in peace.

Be the queen of your lover's heart by having peace with God, and peace with your mate.

Esther pleased the men in her life
Read Esther 2:8b-9.

When she was brought to the king's house and was in the custody of Hegai, keeper of women, she pleased him. He preferred her and her maids unto the best place of the house of women.

How many beautiful women were in this beauty pageant? Imagine the atmosphere in that house of women. Beautiful women without God tend to be proud, haughty, and hateful. Imagine the job Hegai had! Esther must have been a ray of sunshine in that harem of women.

Esther had a close, caring, and respectful relationship with Mordecai, the relative who had taken her in as his own daughter when she was left an orphan. She respected and honored him. She obeyed him even after she was the queen (Esther 2:20). She did the commandment of Mordecai, like as when she was brought up with him.

Esther 2:17 tells us Esther found favor in the king's sight, and he loved her above all the women.

Your husband loves you above all women, right? Proverbs 5:15-20 speaks of the love of husband and wife. Rejoice with the wife of thy youth; let her breasts satisfy thee at all times; be thou ravished also with her love. We are the queen of the home when we love and satisfy our husband.

Do you please your husband? When you were still at home, did you please your dad? Pleasing goes hand in hand with respect. It is of great importance for daughters to respect and please their dad. It is of utmost importance for wives to honor and respect their husband.

I Corinthians 7:34b says the married woman cares about how she may please her husband.

When a marriage goes sour someone no longer respects or cares to please the other.

How Can You Please Your Husband?

Things that seem small and ordinary are very important:

· Give him delicious meals each day.
· Keep the house in decent array.
· Compliment him on how he provides for you.
· Study what you can do to please him. Be creative.
· Give him warm, sexual love, approval, and admiration.
· Be aware of his work and take an interest in it.

A man is better equipped to face the demands and stresses of life when he is satisfied with his wife.

Help your husband by meeting the children's needs. Take time to give them the love, discipline, and attention they need.

A friend shared with me, "My husband loves foot rubs, late night snacks, and an 'I'm anxious to snuggle with you' kind of wife. I try to do that for him. I love to please him," she said. "It pleases him so much when I go with him and we spend time together. Sometimes I will just look at him and think about how much I like him, what I like about him, and I thank God for those things.

"I try to keep things in perspective. What matters most; my relationship with my husband and family, or my housework, sewing, and other things?"

She shared, "I have reaped the blessing of having a husband who loves me and our children dearly, and he has learned to speak my love language. I often must ask him for forgiveness for a bad attitude or unnecessary fussing. He graciously forgives and never holds a grudge. He is just really nice to live with."

What a testimony. What an example to follow.

You too will reap heaps of blessings when you please your spouse. Kindness comes back. He will very likely want to please you too. You will know the peace and contentment that comes from doing the will of God.

Be the queen of your husband's heart. Please him.

Esther fasted and prayed

Scripture does not say she prayed, yet fasting and prayer go together. In a time of crisis she flew to God. God's care of His people is so evident and real in this account, though the name of God is not mentioned in the book of Esther.

Like Esther we need to fast and pray about the problems that come our way.

Fasting is not easy. It is difficult. It is a spiritual discipline. Fasting is not to get your own way. Fasting is a special seeking of God's will. It is to give up the problem to God.

Betty Miller, a counselor at Life Ministries, said, "True fasting grows from a burdened heart which experiences a greater concern for a person, purpose, or vision than for food."

Is There Value in Fasting?

· In the Bible, fasting is expected!!! Matthew 6:16: "Moreover, when ye fast..." It says "*when* ye fast" NOT "*if* ye fast."

· Fasting does not change God's hearing as much as it changes our praying. (I read that all biblical purposes of fasting relate to prayer.)

· There is more power available through fasting! Listen to this verse...referring to casting out demons, Mark 9:29: "And he said unto them, This kind can come forth by nothing, but by prayer and fasting."

· Fasting shows you desire more to know what God wants than your natural desire for food. I think sometimes when we want answers from God, He waits to answer till He sees how desperate we are about this, how much we really need an answer. God answers those who knock...who knock desperately. Fasting is definitely a sign of desperation. Desperation to hear God and to get answers from Him.[13]

Do you pray for your husband each day? Bless him with your daily prayers.

Pray:

- that he would seek God first
- that he would command his children and his house after God
- that he would be fulfilled in his work
- that he would have wisdom for financial decisions
- that he would give your children the care, council, and attention they need

My friend Lois' husband is a tour guide for European Tours. She has had the opportunity to tour Europe numerous times. She has also often stayed home alone with their children.

"How do you cope?" I quizzed her. She said she asks her church family to pray especially for her during that time, and feels that those prayers help so much. Remember to ask others to pray for you when your husband is gone or extra busy.

Lois reminds me of I Peter 3:1: "Be in subjection to your own husband."

Whatever your husband works, he needs your prayers. One minister's wife said, "I like to spend some time in fasting and praying for him when he is preparing for a sermon."

It is a good thing to first pray about our struggles before we talk to our husband or other women. We need to make it a habit to "tell it to Jesus."

Pray and do what you can to bless your husband. Be the queen of his heart. Pray for him daily. Adapt to him. Fit in with his plans.

Esther was a woman of appeal and influence

Do you have influence? What kind of influence are you?

There's a funny little saying that goes like this: "He's the head, and I'm the neck that turns the head." Well, like it or not, you influence your man a lot!

Esther first fasted and prayed to obtain God's favor and wisdom. Then she obtained the favor of the king. She took care to look her best when she came to the king. Speaking very respectfully, she invited him to a banquet. After the king was in a mellow mood from the second sumptuous feast, she presented her request. Esther acted with cunning and courage, asking the king for what she wanted, while continuing to show respect. Her behavior is an amazing example of the use of feminine charm and even weakness to enlist support and authority for a cause!

In Esther 8:5 she said, "If it please the king, and if I have found favor in his sight, and the thing seem right before the king, and I be pleasing in his eyes, let it be written...."

Esther's influence was powerful, saving the lives of many.

If a verse was written about each one of our influence, I wonder how it would read.

Scriptures record many interesting accounts of how women influenced their men. Jezebel: "There was none like unto Ahab, which did sell himself to work wickedness in the sight of the Lord, whom Jezebel his wife stirred up" (I Kings 21:25). Zeresh: Zeresh encouraged Haman to built the gallows for Mordecai...(Esther 5:14). Elizabeth: Zacharias and Elizabeth "were both righteous before God, walking in all the commandments and ordinances of the Lord blameless" (Luke 1:6). Isn't that beautiful?

A true helpmeet is one who cooperates wholeheartedly with her husband in working out the plan of God.

If your husband fills his role in having regular family devotions, express appreciation. Do your best to make it work. Don't be like one woman who was too busy for family worship, or just not cooperative. Finally her husband gave up and had a sharing time Bible story with the children at bedtime.

It is such a joy and a beautiful thing when husband and wife work together to serve the Lord. Man was created for fellowship and companionship. We really need help from above to be a help-meet, to die to self, to be a "yes" woman, a blessing woman, a woman with a kind tongue, and a woman who keeps her vows.

"Wives cannot qualify their husband, but they can disqualify him."

Be the queen of his heart by your godly influence.

Death to self

Esther had to give up all the dreams she had prior to the time she was chosen to go to the king's house. She was beautiful at the core, with a heart of love for God, enabling her to be useful and pleasant in a difficult situation.

Lovingly serving and blessing our men takes a continual death to self. In a Christian marriage a man and a woman place their own needs as secondary to those of their spouse. To marry means that we commit ourselves to not meeting only our own needs, but rather to meet the needs of the other.

There comes a time in most marriages when we will make the choice either to draw apart and go separate ways in our lives or invest in the time and energy it takes to stay close and connected.

For many years if Mark went on a short singing tour with his students I stayed at home. It seemed like I was always pregnant or had a baby or toddler to care for. One spring Mark wanted me to go along on their three-day trip. I didn't want to. Late nights and traveling aren't my favorite thing. I don't like to make arrangements for the children to stay elsewhere. Finally I just knew going along is what I needed to do. We took the youngest one with us. I did enjoy most of the trip, and loved meeting old friends and making some new ones. The children survived without us. Most importantly, it was good for our relationship.

We once had an opportunity to go on a European Tour. Mark had to work hard to persuade me to go. I could tell he badly wanted to. As usual, I was worried about the children. Who could we ask to stay with them? Is it good for them if we leave for so long?

I came to realize that Mark very much wanted to go. I needed to give up and go with him. It was amazing how things fell in place. One of our school teachers, a friend whose influence we valued highly, stayed with some of our children. The children suffered no lasting ill effects from our absence. The trip was informative, interesting, and another jewel of things done together.

If your husband wants to travel, go with him and enjoy it. (Remember, "The world is a book; those who do not travel read only one page!") And just what if, oh horrible thought, he wouldn't want you to go along?

I asked one of my friends how she copes with caring for their three small children while her husband directs their large church chorus. She replied that her husband once said he enjoys directing the chorus so much he hopes he can direct till he dies! She felt if that means so much to her husband, why not support him and allow him to be involved in a worthwhile ministry? She also likes the agreement they have that she and their little boys do not need to attend all chorus programs.

"It is not always easy," she said. "I do want him to do all he can for the Lord, and to excel in what he wants to do. If I am grumpy the evening before he leaves, it affects his practices."

The woman who supports her husband in his ministry is wise! Try to be a "yes" woman, instead of always dragging your feet.

He often needs your presence, and always your love and support. I pray that God would give Mark wisdom to lead our family well. I need to work on being a "yes" woman, being excited about his suggestions, and fitting in with his plans. At the same time he values my input and ideas.

Many years ago the wife of evangelist Charles F. Weigle was sick and tired of her husband's busy schedule. One day when Charles returned home from an evangelistic crusade he found a note left by his wife of many years. The note said she was leaving him. She had had enough of an evangelist's wife's life.

Charles went through a terrible time of despondency and discouragement. He felt no one really cared for him anymore.

Gradually, slowly, his faith was restored. He again became active in Christian ministry. Out of that experience of heartbreak he wrote the song, "No One Ever Cared for Me Like Jesus."

The late Roman Mullet once said, "The work of God is not without sacrifice." Are we willing to let our husbands serve in whatever way God has called them? Do we accept their work, and support what God has called them to do?

A friend related this, "Soon after my husband was ordained, I was complaining to my mother-in-law that it is hard to accept that my husband was the chosen one. That was 26 years ago. I still remember her response. With tears in her eyes, she said, 'Be thankful your husband is qualified to be in the ministry.'" Her husband was not living for God. He was not in the church.

My friend continued, "Today I am thankful my husband is doing what God called him to do. I wouldn't want the experience of being married to a rebellious man."

We all need to get in the habit of praising the Lord, being thankful, and focusing on the good. That helps you and your spouse so very much!!

Lovingly serving and blessing your husband takes a continual death to self, a "yes" to God, a "yes" to serving. It will bear the fruit of a husband who gives you the love and adoration your heart longs for, the fruit of a happy, contented, and successful husband in most cases.

Be the queen of his heart by dying to self and saying "Yes" to him.

Be a blessing woman with a kind tongue

King Ahasuerus must have liked being with Esther, for he held out the golden scepter when she came to him.

A man will almost inevitably melt at the feet of a woman who blesses him and lovingly serves him with her kind deeds and words. He will do almost anything to make her happy. As we look to God and His Word to meet our needs, we can be blessing women, blessing our husband, family, and others with refreshing kindness.

Ways to be a blessing woman:
· Praise your husband
· Pray for him
· Talk about his good points in front of others
· Give loving notes
· Be glad to see him and welcome him joyfully when he comes home
· Be aware of him
· Take care of things that irritate him
· Respect his wishes

Men long for and need their wife's approval and respect. Give him what he needs; don't make him long for someone else.

Sometimes before we fall asleep, Mark and I will discuss blessings from our day. The other night I asked him, "Was there anything nice about your day?" He replied, "You!" That blessed me so much; those words have sung in my mind often since then.

Men interact in a tough world day after day. They need a calm, refreshing refuge, a shady, fruitful tree that is blessing them with kindness. They don't need a shriveled, self-centered, dissatisfied, irritable woman who will drive them away.

The cook for a harvest crew in Oregon was told, "We don't care if your food turns out or not, but whatever you do, don't be grouchy. After we worked hard in the fields all day, the last thing we want to see is a grouchy cook."

That is a concept women do well to take note of. Men often face a hard, difficult world. If we want to relate peacefully with them, we must recognize that they are looking to us for a haven from the storm they have faced all day. They are looking to us for encouragement and refreshment.

One of women's biggest struggles is their own slippery tongue. Only with God's help can our tongue be tamed. Be a blessing woman with a kind tongue. Remember Proverbs 31:26: "In her tongue is the law of kindness."

Remember your vows; share with your husband

Esther did her best to bless her marriage. She was not looking for someone else.

On your wedding day you promised to take the man by your side, to love and cherish him in health and in sickness, in prosperity and in adversity, share with him the joys and sorrows of life, exercise patience, kindness, and forbearance toward him, and live with him in peace, as becometh a faithful Christian wife; and, forsaking all others, keep yourself only unto him, as long as ye both shall live.

It doesn't matter how good you think your marriage is today; there is always room to grow and improve.

To bless and help each other we must communicate. It is strange how you can live and sleep together, yet feel you are in a dirth for lack of time to talk.

Men do not think like women, and most times they really don't know what we want unless we tell them. We need to learn to lovingly share our feelings.

Once I was preparing a talk for teachers' wives. It was very important to me that Mark read my notes. He didn't get it done. I placed the notes on his desk in plain sight and told him, "If you don't take time to read them it will be a point of offense to me."

Finally he read my notes and penciled on them words of encouragement for me.

We must communicate to have a good marriage. A woman's tendency is to fret when he doesn't live up to your expectations. If you want him to help you, tell him. If you need something, let him know. Also, take time to ask him what he likes from you.

A minister's wife said when her husband is extra busy and she needs to talk, she asks him to go on a walk after supper. "If I sit back and think he should know when I need to talk it leads to disappointment," she shared.

Remember your vows; share with your husband.

Your home is in essence your palace. You, the mother, are the queen. It is a huge task; a calling that can be overwhelming. Raising a family is no child's play, but work for men and women who are strong in the Lord.

Remember: Be the queen of your husband's heart by:
· living in peace with God and your mate
· pleasing him
· praying for him daily
· your godly influence
· dying to self and saying "Yes"
· blessing him with kind deeds and words
· remembering your vows; sharing with him

Ruth 1:9: "The Lord grant you that ye may find rest, each of you in the house of her husband." The Greek definition of rest is a quiet and a settled spot, peaceful repose, comfortable.

As we follow God's plan for our marriages and our homes, He will bless us with peace in our hearts and peace in our homes. God gives rest—a quiet, peaceful, and settled spot—a home that is a haven.

· ·

Esther did what she could for God where He placed her! She was faithful. What will you do where God placed you? The closing story for this chapter is about Crist and Rachel Beiler. I value their example of faithfulness and their attitude of praise throughout life. At the end of their days they were ready to meet their Savior.

PRAISE THE LORD FOR HIS GOODNESS

What is more beautiful than an aged man and his wife, their hair all snowy white, who have lived in love and peace since their youthful wedding day?

Together they have weathered the storms of life and lived in faithfulness.

Hand in hand, they are still walking together, toward a wondrous sunset, anticipating their final rest and heavenly home.

What is more sad than the vast numbers of homes today that are full of bleeding and bruised hearts, broken vows, and broken children? The children are broken, bitter, bruised, and betrayed because Dad and Mom no longer love one another. The choices that are made in youth profoundly affect the rest of life.

"Choose you this day whom you will serve; as for me and my house, we will serve the Lord" (Joshua 24:15).

Crist's gnarled, wrinkled hands lovingly stroked the pages of his precious Bible. "Oh, that men would praise the Lord for his goodness, and for his wonderful works to the children of men." He murmured his favorite verse as he reverently closed the Bible. His wife sat nearby contentedly rocking.

"Rachel," Crist said, "we are so richly blessed. God has given us sixty-five years of life together." He looked at her tenderly. "I remember how you supported me when God called me to the ministry. You have been a wonderful companion and a godly mother to our eleven children. Marrying you was one of the best decisions I ever made."

Rachel's face beamed with the contentment and joy that comes from a godly life and a faithful husband who made her feel his love by his kind words and deeds.

As usual that night before they retired, they knelt together. "And when you are through with us in this life," Crist prayed, "would you be pleased to receive us to glory without the loss of one. In Jesus' name I pray with thanksgiving. Amen."

The next day Crist heard his wife coughing again. Rachel had had problems with asthma for many years, but when Crist brought her home from another doctor's appointment he was heartsick. The doctor had said Rachel had pneumonia; her lungs were worn out. It was so difficult to know that their parting was inevitable.

"It is such a lamentable fact," Crist mused. "Some people *want* to leave their partners, while others *have* to."

Rachel was ill for two months before God called her home. Every family member and spouse took turns caring for their mother around the clock. Mother was cheerful and had few complaints. The family was blessed by working together and caring for her. It was something they would never regret.

Those last weeks were hallowed ground to the children, and beautiful with God's love, peace, and presence. Rachel often talked about heaven. She quoted many Scriptures, and in a clear voice sang songs of praise to God. That was a special gift. The family had not heard their mother sing for years, due to her asthma and shortness of breath.

"Oh, is this morning," Rachel said one day. "I thought the Lord was coming to take me home last night. Tell Him not to forget me tonight."

Eight months earlier Rachel's daughter Lill had died after a battle with cancer. A few days before Rachel's death, her family was gathered around her, when she looked up and said, "Oh, it is so beautiful up there; the grass is lush and green; the flowers are so lovely. There are countless children running about and they are all so happy. They don't even need any toys to play with.

"And oh, oh, there is Lill! She looks so beautiful, and she has such a happy smile. Where is Floyd? Tell him how happy Lill is."

One day she saw some of the grandchildren silently shedding tears. "Don't weep for me," Rachel said. "Weep for the next generation. I know where I am going."

Rachel was bedfast her last three days. In her last hour her breathing was so labored and heavy that the bed shook. Her daughter Alta told her, "Mom, it's okay to go." Alta prayed out loud, "Lord, take her home."

Later Alta said it was an awesome experience to stand at the bedside of her dying mother, knowing she was being ushered into eternity. It was beautiful because she knew her mother was ready to meet the Lord.

"Yea, though I walk through the valley of the shadow of death, I will fear no evil, for thou art with me" (Psalm 23:4).

End Notes

1. Ray Vander Laan Seminar: The Jewish Gospel in a Greek World

2. Randy Alcorn, *Safely Home* pg. 89, Tyndale House Publishers

3. Rosalind Goforth, *Jonathan Goforth*, Bethany House Publishers

4. Elizabeth Prentiss, *Stepping Heavenward*, Barbour Publishing, pg. 315

5. Elizabeth Elliot, *A Chance to Die, The Life and Legacy of Amy Charmichael*

6. Tom Friesen, June 2004 *Sword and Trumpet*

7. Mary June Glick, March 2004 *Calvary Messenger*

8. Liz Lapp, *Committed to the Covenant*, 2007 Christian Light Publications.

9. *Bartletts Familiar Quotations,* pg. 634

10. Sue Poorman Richards and Lawrence O. Richards, *Women of the Bible,*
    Nashville, Tenn., Thomas Nelson, 2003, pg. 54

11. William T. Ellis, *The Man and His Message*

12. *Bible Readings for the Home*, pg. 721

13. "Is There Value in Fasting?" Mary Lynita Beachy

Mary Ellen, with her husband Mark, currently lives in Dundee, Ohio. She is a busy mother of six. Singing for tourists, operating a greenhouse, and working in the garden are some of her favorite activities.

Mary Ellen enjoys writing and often says that God gives her the inspiration for a story. Her desire is that through her writing, God would be honored and women would be encouraged in their walk with God.

About My Mom

"You did a good job!"
"Thanks so much for baking that bread!"
"You are such a neat seamstress."

It is said that most people receive ten criticisms for every compliment. Not so for us. Mom specializes in encouraging and praying for her children.

Some frequent quotes from Mom. . .
"Read your Bible before you read anything else in the morning."
"You catch more flies with honey than with vinegar."
"Have you talked to the Lord about it?"

Mom grew up on the eastern shore of Maryland. While in grade school, she enjoyed doing extra studying on subjects of interest. Later she taught school for four years.

—*A daughter, Mary Lynita Beachy*